Low Carb Instant Pot Cookbook

To Rapidly Lose Weight, Regain 100% Confidence and Have a Better Life

81 Flavored& Easy Low Carb Instant Pot Recipes
(Bonus: 14 Days Low Carb Diet Meal Plan)

By Chef Watson

Disclaimer

All rights Reserved. By no means should any content of this publication or the information in it be quoted or replicated in any other form whether through printing, scanning, photocopying or otherwise, without any form of written permission from the copyright holder.

Table of Contents

About The Book...8

Introduction..10

CHAPTER 1: AN OVERVIEW OF THE LOW CARB DIET PLAN......12

    What Is A Low Carb Diet?..12

    History of the Low Carb Diet..13

    The Health Benefits of the Low Carb Diet..13

    Permitted and Non Permitted Foods in the Low Carb Diet Plan.................13

    How Can Low Carb Diet Enhances Weight loss..14

    23 Tips to Attaining a Successful Low Carb Diet Plan................................14

    Frequently Asked Question...16

    Who Should Partake in the Low Carb Diet..16

    The Challenges Faced When Following a Low Carb Diet..........................16

    CAUTION..17

    Low Carb Diet Hacks...17

    8 Low Carb Diet Myths..18

Chapter 2: THE INSTANT POT...21

    What Is An Instant Pot?..21

    Origin of the Instant Pot...22

    Benefits of an Instant Pot..22

    How to Maintain the Instant Pot..22

    Rules in Using the Instant Pot..23

    How to Choose a Good Instant Pot..23

    Where to Buy an Instant Pot?...24

CHAPTER 3: 81 LOW CARB INSTANT POT RECIPES.......................25

    15 Tasty Breakfasts..25

1. Egg Muffins with Vegetables..25
2. Savory Breakfast Muffins...26
3. Yummy Breakfast...28
4. Boiled Egg for Breakfast..29
5. Pressure Cooker Breakfast Quinoa..30
6. Delicious Pancake in Instant Pot..31
7. Eggs and Bacon Cups..32
8. Avocado Bread..33
9. Scramble Egg in Instant Pot..35
10. Instant Pot Berries and Cream Breakfast Cake..36
11. Easy Two Ingredients Jam in Instant Pot..38
12. Breakfast Cobbler..39
13. Breakfast Porridge..40
14. Simple and Delicious Muffin Recipes 41
15. Instant Pot Bacon Ranch Potatoes...42

16 Mouth-Watering Soups..44

1. Instant Pot Squash Soup...44
2. Mushroom Soup...45
3. Spinach Soup..46
4. Spicy Barley Soup...47
5. Vegetable Soup...48
6. Spicy Chicken Soup..49
7. Oriental Soup with Noodles and Chicken..51
8. Lamb Soup with Barley..52
9. Buffalo Chicken Soup...53
10. Carrot Soup..54
11. Instant Pot Broccoli Cheddar Soup..56
12. Vidalia onion Soup..57
13. Dilled Carrot Soup...58

14. Garlic Soup...59

15. Split-Pea Soup with Ham...60

16. Down-Home Soup...61

10 Vegetable Recipes..63

1. Veggies Risotto...63

2. Coconut Cabbage in Instant Pot...64

3. Zucchini Casserole..66

4. Simple Slow Cook Recipe...67

5. Sweet and Sour Beet Roots..68

6. Hearty Chowder..69

7. Garden Stew...70

8. Easy Cheesy Vegetables..71

9. A Simple Cooking Recipe..72

10. The Celery and Cauliflower Recipe...73

10 Graceful Meats..75

1. Chicken Adobo..75

2. BBQ Ribs...76

3. Instant Pot Roasted Beef..77

4. Ginger and Soy Chicken...78

5. Simple Beef Stew..79

6. Coconut Beef Curry...80

7. Beetroot and Beef Stew..82

8. Steak and Gravy...83

9. Beef with Apricots...84

10. Gravy Chicken...85

10 Great Lunches...87

1. Fish and Tomato Stew..87

2. Instant Pot Fettuccine with Seafood...88

3. Shrimp and Vegetable Stew...89

4. Slow-Cooker Pork Chops..90

5. Pork and Squash Ragout..91

6. Ginger Pumpkin Chicken Soup..92

7. Zucchini Casserole Recipe...93

8. Curry-Spiced Nuts..94

9. Eggplant Caviar..95

10. Instant Pot Chicken..96

10 Yummy Desserts..98

1. Gingerbread Cake...98

2. Chocolate Chip Peanut Butter Cake..99

3. Five-Layer Bars...100

4. Easy Brownies..102

5. Lemon Cream Cheese Bites..103

6. Rhubarb-Strawberry Compote...104

7. Baked Apples..105

8 Chocolate Fondue..106

9. Winter Fruit Compote..107

10. Rum Raisin Caramel Fondue..108

10 Flavored Dinners..109

1. Karelian Ragout..109

2. Three-Meat Goulash...110

3. Family Beef Stew..111

4. Plain Meat Loaf..112

5. Lemon Meat Loaf...113

6. Pork Stew with Prunes...115

7. Teriyaki Chicken Wings..116

8. Country-Style Ribs with Sauce...117

9. Moroccan Lamb Stew...118

10. Meat Goulash..119

Chapter 4: 14 Days Meal Plan..121
    The Main Aim of Writing This Chapter...122
    Useful Tips for the 2 Weeks Meal Plan Preparation...........................122
    (2-weeks) 14 Days Meal Plan..122

Conclusion..126

About The Book

Are you fed up with your overweight? Do you feel lack of confidence because of your obesity? Are you looking for a diet for weight loss? Do you want to have delicious foods without paying too much time everyday? This book will solve all of above questions! It is not just a cookbook, it is a complete guide of Low Carb diet and Instant Pot Cooking. It is a perfect companion for your daily cooking!

So what benefits will you get by following a low carb diet?
1. Helps In a Swift Reduction In Appetite.
2. Helps To Lose Weight Effectively.
3. Lowers The Blood Triglycerides.
4. Increases The Levels Of Good Cholesterol (Hdl).
5. Reduces The Blood Sugar Levels.
6. 6. Reduces Hypertension.
7. Helps Improve Brain Disorders.
8. Gives More Energy.
9. Improves Health And Fitness.
10. More And More...

Besides, by following this book, you will know:
1. Everything About Low Carb Diet
2. Foods You Should Eat/ Avoid
3. Overview Of Instant Pot
4. 81 Delicious And Easy Instant Pot Recipes
5. A 2- Week Healthy Meal Plan
6. More and More...

Out there in our world today, we see a lot of overweight people, in churches, our workplaces, grocery stores and so on. Most of them often do make attempt towards fighting the weight problem, but often a times do fail. What most of them obviously always fail to know is that, for anyone to see a positive result in weight loss, you have to follow a good and efficient diet plan alongside a proper exercise routine. One of the most productive methods of losing weight is through adopting a certain diet plan. Many people follow numerous diet plans, hoping to lose weight, but still fail to get their dream body just because they adopt the wrong kind of diet plan. So, if you are in search of an effective dieting remedy, that will help you lose a great deal of weight and invariably keep you healthy, fit, and active, regain confidence, then this book is certainly for you.

For some people, weight loss could be very tedious, but the truth is, it's not that much of a stress. Anyone can lose weight, have a sexy looking bikini body and live a healthy lifestyle. The only thing needed is for one to be precise, because weight loss processes are more about addressing the key issues in an appropriate manner, so that the weight will be under control by the person and at the same time won't have to leave the person worrying about being overweight or losing control.

The main aim of this book is to help people lose weight, regain confidence and stay fit permanently by introducing them into a low carb diet plan. The book also provides solutions to all the matters concerning weight loss. And most essentially, all the recipes included in this book will make you have a taste of healthy and tasty foods that will invariably nourish your body. If you are sick and tired of following unsuccessful diet plans that at the end of the day amount to nothing, then this book is all you could ever ask for.

The book contains 81 delicious and mouthwatering low carb instant pot recipes. If you have never used an instant pot before, then don't fret, as we have dedicated a chapter to enlighten you on the introduction and maintenance of the instant pot. If you're a busy person who finds it hard to carve out time to prepare meals, then you can take advantage of this appliance to save time, fuel and energy.

Meantime, all of these recipes are all well chosen and proven to be top recipes. All you need to do is just buy the ingredients in your local market and put them into the instant pot, then wait for some minutes you will have a very nutritional and mouth-watering dish. Hope you will like this book and get the benefits you want!

At the end of the book, we have made a healthy and perfect Low Carb Diet meal plan, you can follow it. You will get amazing result in near future!

N/B: All the recipes are made from natural, organic, low carb, and whole foods. So, let the journey begin.

Introduction

The book "Low Carb Instant Pot Cookbook To Rapidly Lose Weight, Regain 100% Confidence and Have a Better Life" is a cookbook that targets people who wish to have a taste of some delicious and healthy low carb instant pot recipes for the purpose of weight loss and living a healthier lifestyle.

Unarguably a low carb diet helps you to stay in shape without adding extra pounds to your body. Obesity is one of the biggest issues faced by millions of people around the world. When it comes to weight loss and diet, many people feel unmotivated and get frustrated just by thinking of it. So, if you are struggling to lose some pounds of weight or want to live a much healthier lifestyle, then this cookbook is for you. Low Carb diet is an effective and natural way of eating with low carb high fat foods.

Having a fixed diet plan and exercising sounds very easy, but the hardest part is in implementing them, because that is where the real work is. And so with that, we aim at main making people understand the effectiveness of low Carb intake in the process of weight loss. Many people believe that the higher the percentage of fat in their diet the more likely they are to having serious health issues like obesity, heart disease and much more. While this may be true, as many studies have recommended that people should reduce their intake of fat by less than 30 percent in total, still notwithstanding it is advisable even by many health professionals to make use of a low Carb diet plan to ensure better health, weight loss, and fitness. Many studies conducted in recent years have shown the effectiveness of the low Carb diet over many other diet plans. The main outcome measurements were in cholesterol level, obesity, blood sugar, and Triglycerides. These studies were conducted on people having health problems, which included obesity, type II diabetes, and metabolic syndrome.

The first study was conducted by **Foster GD, et al.** a randomly selected trial of a low-carbohydrate diet for obesity . **New England Journal of Medicine, 2003.** This study had about 63 individuals on a low Carb diet for 12 months. The results however showed a 7.3% loss of total body weight in the patients. Moreover, the patients had greater improvement in their

blood triglycerides and HDL.
(http://www.nejm.org/doi/full/10.1056/NEJMoa022207)

The second study was conducted by Samaha FF, et al. a low-carbohydrate diet in comparison with a low-fat diet in tackling severe obesity. **New England Journal of Medicine, 2003. The study lasted** for 6 months, and at the end about 132 individuals with severe obesity were recommended the low Carb diet. Many of the individuals following the diet were having metabolic syndrome or type II diabetes as well.
(http://www.nejm.org/doi/full/10.1056/NEJMoa022637)

The study results showed that:
1. Triglycerides went down by 38 mg/DL.
2. Insulin sensitivity improved very prominently.
3. Fasting Blood sugar went down by 26 mg/DL.
4. Insulin went down by 27%.

Also in 2012 a study was carried out by Guldbrand, et al. Concerning a type 2 diabetes, a comparison was made between a randomly selected group of people who were advised to follow a low-carbohydrate diet as it transiently improves Glycaemic and a group advised to follow just a low-fat diet producing a similar weight loss. **Diabetologia, 2012.** The results showed that the low Carb group had greater reductions in BMI and other biomarker improvements.
(https://link.springer.com/article/10.1007%2Fs00125-012-2567-4)

So in a nutshell, if you want a flat stomach, reduction in weight, regain confidence, and to live a healthier life then this book will actually be your savior.

CHAPTER 1: AN OVERVIEW OF THE LOW CARB DIET PLAN

If you are a busy person, it could be frustrating at most times as you will often find yourself not being able to do carryout some certain tasks like having enough time to prepare meals that will maintain your weight and glucose level in a good way. Well if you are among such group of persons, then I am glad to announce to you that there is finally a way out of this frustration as this book will reduce the whole processes to its simplest and quickest form, and improve your health condition provided you follow the low carb diet properly. In today's fast and changing society, we all get busy at some point and do need meals that are healthy and easy to prepare. For us, the solution is hidden in junk food choices which are not healthy enough to keep us fit. All the junk foods, artificial flavors, and processed food items are the major causes of bad health and obesity, which often do leads to severe disease like heart attack, diabetes, headache, kidney stones, etc.

Nowadays, millions of people in the world are suffering from obesity, hypertension, and diabetes. The sickness worsens when proper care and attention to address it are not available which often results in life threatening diseases .Taking all that into account, it is highly recommended to have the low Carb diet plan as it does not only guard you off this fatal diseases but also reduces your weight and blood sugar. The Low Carb diet plan is the most efficient method to all the obese people, as well as those who want to lose some extra pounds. The plan includes low Carb fruits, vegetables, meat, fish, poultry, nuts, and unsweetened items. Before we proceed, let us clear the air on what the Low Carb Diet is.

What Is A Low Carb Diet?

This is a very simple diet plan that limits the carbohydrates found in most of the starchy fruits, vegetables, and grains. The main emphasis is on food with high protein, fiber, and fat.

History of the Low Carb Diet
The history of this diet goes back to 1972 when a cardiologist named Robert C. Atkins created a diet plan that restricted carbs while emphasizing on protein and fat. His basic purpose in creating this plan was to change an eating habit to enhance good health, weight loss, and fitness. According to Dr. Atkins, this diet is a healthy lifelong approach to eating. It helps maintain weight, cholesterol, sugar level, and blood pressure.

The Health Benefits of the Low Carb Diet
Some proven benefits of the low Carb diet plan are:
- Low Carb diet lowers the hunger pangs in a good way. It helps in a swift reduction in appetite.
- Eating fewer calories help to lose weight effectively.
- Blood triglycerides are fat molecules in blood and are known for causing heart diseases. Low Carb diets effectively lower the blood triglycerides.
- Increases the levels of Good Cholesterol (HDL).
- Reduces the blood sugar levels.
- Reduces hypertension.
- Helps improve brain disorders.
- Gives more energy.
- Improves health and fitness.

Permitted and Non Permitted Foods in the Low Carb Diet Plan

Non Permitted
1. Bread and grains
2. Sugar breakfast cereal
3. Starchy fruits
4. Starchy vegetables
5. Beer
6. White sugar
7. Maple syrup
8. Honey
9. Agave nectar

⑩ Sweetened yogurt
⑪ Milk

Permitted
- Unsweetened almond milk
- Unsweetened coconut milk
- Small amount of lentils and beans
- Olive oil
- Nut oil
- Vinegar
- Low Carb fruits
- Low Carb Vegetables
- Meat
- Eggs
- Natural yogurt
- Small amount of wheat

How Can Low Carb Diet Enhances Weight loss

The low Carb diet is all about cutting Carbs from the meal, invariably causing your kidney to start shedding excess water. From the water loss most people lose a lot of weight at the start which is actually water weight that reaches up to 5-10 pounds. After the first week, it will then focus on shredding fat from your fat stores. The low Carb diet helps in reducing ones appetite and invariably causing weight loss without the need for calories control. So that means you can eat as much as you wish to and still feel satisfied as well. In addition, the low Carb diet also helps in reducing the insulin level which store fats in the body, and by so doing leading to a reduction in the body weight.

23 Tips to Attaining a Successful Low Carb Diet Plan

Along with a healthy low Carb diet plan, timing is the most important factor. First, it is important to know the type of meal you want to prepare. If you follow a proper meal plan, it will surely have a significant effect on your overall health. Another important thing that you will need to take care of is the timing of when you will be eating your meal. Eat properly and on time as it will help speed up your metabolism rate more effectively, and prevent the body from increasing its fat storage.

1. Reduce the amount of added sugar and other carbs in your meal.
2. Calculate your Carbs percentage using a handy crab counter.
3. Keep calories as low as possible, because too much will slow down the weight loss process.
4. Eat regularly and keep starvation at bay.
5. Include protein in your everyday meal.
6. Eat more vegetables and fruits.
7. Drink a good amount of water.
8. Enjoy drinking tea or coffee, as it both helps in getting rid of water weight.
9. Take a daily multivitamin supplement.
10. Indulge yourself in any physical activity and exercise.
11. Keep track of your success on a diet.
12. Decide on your choices of meal before shopping in the grocery.
13. Eat breakfast as early as possible after waking up.
14. Appreciate personal food choices as well. There is no need to go hard on any diet.
15. Check the food labels before buying any food item for extra sugar content.
16. Go for organic food items.
17. Avoid artificial flavors and preservatives.
18. Say a big "NO" to sodas and canned juices while on the low Carb diet. You can substitute these beverages with healthy homemade smoothies and juice made from low Carb vegetable and fruits.
19. Concentrate more on leafy vegetable, low Carb fruits, vegetables, fish and white meat based meal plans.
20. Chose the healthiest oil for cooking that is cholesterol free.
21. Consume a low Carb, high protein, and a high fiber diet.
22. Go low on overall carbohydrates.
23. Always fill half your plate with fruits and vegetables.

Frequently Asked Question

1. How many Carb one should eat on low Carb diet?
The Institute of Medicine recommends a dietary allowance of carbohydrate at 70 grams daily for 2000 calorie meal plan.

2. Can you drink coffee or tea while on a low Carb diet?
Yes, but keep added sugar at bay.

3. Can you eat nuts on the low Carb Diet?
Not in the first week.

4. Can a vegan follow low Carb diet?
Yes, it can be followed by vegan or vegetarians.

5. Can lentil be part of a low Carb diet?
Yes, but in limit.

Who Should Partake in the Low Carb Diet

Adding less Carb in one's daily meal can make a huge difference to your overall health. It helps in reducing weight, lowering insulin level, kidney disease and much more. The low Carb diet is strongly recommended for:

1. People with diabetes
2. People with kidney diseases
3. People with obesity
4. People with any sort of inflammation
5. Older and middle age people
6. People with hypertension

The Challenges Faced When Following a Low Carb Diet

When following the low Carb diet plan the most common challenges that most of us are likely to face are:

- The Family eating at different times
- The differences in food choices
- Redundant meal menu
- Medical needs

- Life philosophy needs
- Budget and time

It is important for one to develop the willpower to resist all the sweet treats and high Carb meals. It's important to always keep in mind the overall calorie intake. The core practice of eating healthy in low Carb meals is the pyramid to an optimal fitness and health.

CAUTION

All the recipes that are included in our meal plan responds differently to each and every individual, so it's best to consult your doctor before starting a low Carb diet. From time to time visit your doctor to monitor the changes in your blood sugar and weight.

Low Carb Diet Hacks

Below are some low Carb diet hacks, which help you to choose some basic ingredients to start a meal plan.

Swap these food items	*For these food items*
Sodas and juices	Milk, water and lemon
Burger and French fries	Salads and bun less burgers
Toast and sandwich s	Lettuces wrap and egg wraps
Snacks	Meat, vegetables, and cheese
Processed meat	Organic meat
Ice-cream	Organic and natural yogurt or cakes
Sweets	Chocolate
Cocktail	Red wine
Flour	Almond flour or coconut flour
Crumbs	Grounded Almonds
Margarine	Butter or ghee
Icing	Cream cheese frosting
Sugar	Stevia
Potatoes	Cauliflower

Jam	Berries or fruits
Rice	Cauliflower rice
Processed yogurt	Natural yogurt
Cereal	Eggs, bacon
Milk	Nut milk
Frozen meal	Fresh food items
High Carb fruits	Low Carb Fruits
High Carb vegetables	Low Carb vegetables

8 Low Carb Diet Myths

Despite being a successful plan for effective weight loss and a healthy lifestyle, there are numerous amounts of misconceptions and myths about low Carb diet. Some people believe that low Carb diet is a complete human diet plan and that one should adopt it for better health. While many others think that it is a "fad" diet which is not suitable for human beings due to the adverse effect it has on the body on the long run. Here is the list of the most common myths.

1. It Is a Known as a Fad Diet Plan

The word fad has a lot of meanings. Most people use it to tag a diet plan that they do not deem as being efficient. The low Carb diet was used as a weight loss diet plan, which enjoyed a short popularity; and as such today, a lot of people label the low Carb diet a fad diet. Logically this is erroneous, as there are numerous studies carried out in the past that shows the effectiveness of this diet. It is a well-known & approved diet plan that is being adopted by millions of people for decades now. If we carry out a research about the diet, we will find out that in 1863, a book was published solely for it that sold a million copies worldwide. It is a diet plan that has been in existence for a while now and has been supported by many health professionals, by so doing countering the erroneous tag of it being a Fad diet.

2. It Is Difficult To Follow
Many people are of the view that it is a very difficult diet to follow as it restricts commonly found food items from being consumed. This makes people feel uncomfortable, causing them to abandon the low Carb diet, which often ends in weight gaining still. While this maybe a reasonable argument, it is important to note that almost all the diet plan restricts food items. Some restrict fat, some strict macro nutrients, and others limit calories. The good thing about the low-Carb diet is that it reduces hunger, so that you can still eat until you are satisfied and invariably manage to lose weight at the same time.

3. The Weight You Lose Is Water Weight Not Fats
The human body stores a lot of carbs in the liver and muscle called glycogen. Glycogen is used to provide glucose to the body which also helps in binding some certain percentage of water. When you stop eating carbs, this storage drops, and your body in turn loses water weight. The low-Carb diet causes reduction in insulin levels which results in making the kidney to lose excess of amount of water and sodium. That single mechanism is the reason why it leads to a reduction in water weight. In addition, the studies suggest that this diet also leads to the reduction in fat, especially from the liver and abdomen.

4. Low-Carb Diet Is Bad For the Heart
The Low-Carb diets are high in fat and low in carbs. Many of us think that they are detrimental to the heart. However, many studies have shown that fat or cholesterol has no adverse effect on the heart functions.

5. Low-Carb Diets Is Successful Because We Eat Lesser Calories
Many of us believe that when we eat less, we lose weight easily; this is only true to some extent. But on a low-Carb diet, weight loss happens almost instantaneously. We feel much fuller and satiated, that we eat less without counting the calories intake. The art of reduction in appetite in the low-carb diet serves as the most effective method to restricting calories intake. And also it is important to note that the Low-Carb diets digestion benefits goes far beyond the calories.

6. It Reduces Our Plant Food Intake
It is a misconception, that reducing Carb makes you eat fewer plant foods. In reality, you can eat a lot of vegetables, nuts, berries, and seeds. But remember, not to exceed 50 g per day.

7. The Brain Needs Glucose
Many people are of the notion that the brain cannot work properly without carbs and that the brain needs 130 grams of carbs each day to function properly. While this is partially true because some brain cells do need glucose to get proactive, that notwithstanding the other parts of the brain are solely dependent on the ketones to get active. If carbohydrates are in short supply, then a significant part of the brain uses ketones instead of glucose. So, here the metabolic track known as gluconeogenesis gets imported where it produces glucose from protein.

8. It Affects Our Physical Performance
Many sportsmen and athletes eat high-Carb diet meal and are healthy. The reduction in Carbs can lead to low performance, of which will only last temporarily until the body gets used to it with time.

Chapter 2: THE INSTANT POT

What Is An Instant Pot?

An Instant pot is just a single appliance with multifunctional features. It can perform the task of the steamer, electric pressure cooker, warming pot and rice cooker. It speeds up the cooking process by using 70 percent less of energy. And now many manufacturers have ventured into the production of this appliance, which is smart, time-saving and is used by millions of people around the world. So if you are a type with a very tight work schedule, then this appliance is the right choice for you. The instant pot uses a pattern of cooking meals in a vessel that is sealed properly, holding the steam inside the pot below a preset pressure. As the water boiling point increases, so does the pressure increases as well. The built up pressure allows the temperature to rise as well, thus making the cooking process quicker.

The instant pot cooking technique is best suitable to people who would rather prefer a time saving meal, as it's quicker and saves a lot of time, making the preparation of a low carb meal less cumbersome. But there things you will need to know before you start using the instant pot, it is important to know the essentials like, how to release the steam and the function of the buttons.

First look at the buttons:
1. To change the time press + or – keys.
2. The ADJUST button changes the cooking temperature.
3. The PRESSURE button changes the pressure from low to high during cooking.
4. The MANUAL setting adjusts the cooking from low to high pressure using the pressure button.
5. To sauté, press the SAUTE button. It automatically adjusts to normal, when we press it, so if you want more or less heat you can use ADJUST button.
6. A SLOW COOK button is used for slow cooking. Here you can adjust the heat using the ADJUST button.
7. STEAM button is used to steam the meal.

8. When cooking a meat, chicken, and soup the heat and temperature requirements are different, that can be adjusted from low to high pressure by using PRESSURE button.

There are two types of the release option in an instant pot. One is the natural release, and other is the quick release. The natural release is when the timer goes off and you let the steam to escape without doing anything. Almost 10 minutes of natural release is required before opening the pot. In the quick release, you release the handle by turning it from sealing to venting to quick release the steam.

Origin of the Instant Pot
The instant pot was invented by Denis Papin a physicist from France in 1679. It was widely used as a household appliance during World War 2, as then the people realized its capability of saving time and energy.

Benefits of an Instant Pot
    1. It is a convenient appliance whose primary function is to reduce one's cooking time.
    2. It helps preserve the nutritional value with great flavor.
    3. It is a clean and effective way of preparing a meal.
    4. It presents one with a pleasant cooking experience.
    5. It is an effective energy device to use.
    6. It is a safe and reliable device.

How to Maintain the Instant Pot
    1. Before cleaning the instant pot, it is necessary to unplug the appliance from the power source.
    2. Always separate the lid and interior for a perfect cleaning process.
    3. Hand-wash the appliance.
    4. Hand-wash the lid with warm soapy water.
    5. Remove the steam-release handle.
    6. Always remove the anti-block shield of the instant pot.

7. Remove the float valve and sealing ring.
8. Then properly wash the inner pot and rack.
9. When you are done cooking, remove the steam release handle.
10. Give it some time to let the steam release.
11. To remove bad odors from a pressure cooker, wash it with water mixed with baking soda.

Rules in Using the Instant Pot

Although the instant pot is a safe cooking appliance to use, still there are some important hints that will help you maximize it for a better performance.

1. Never leave the house while the instant pot is on power.
2. It is advisable not to pressurize any fries in the instant pot.
3. To maintain the pressure while cooking in an instant pot always put a minimum of 1 cup water.
4. Do not fill the instant pot to the brim with grains. Allocate it some space as the food will eventually rise while cooking. The maximum line is usually printed on the instant pot.
5. Keep the inner part of the pot clean.
6. The instant pot silicone sealing ring needs to be replaced every 15-20 months. So it's best to keep the extras.
7. Before starting the cooking process, inspect the sealing ring to make sure that it is well seated in the rack.
8. The anti block shield should be mounted properly on the steam release pipe.

How to Choose a Good Instant Pot

Identifying a good instant pot has been one of the challenges many people have faced in the course of carrying out the low carb diet plan. There are several options available in the market where various manufacturers strive to give you the best quality but in turn makes the buying choices more complicated. It is advisable that you buy the instant pot according to their needs. The function, size, and version should be considered while purchasing the instant pot.

Where to Buy an Instant Pot?

Once you buy your instant pot, you will fall in love with this handy device. It is one magical device that converts an average cooking pattern into a professional one. With the sales doubling over the last few years, the instant pot is the fastest growing kitchen appliance. In 2009, after the instant pot was debuted, it became the first brand to hit North America. According to studies, in 2010 more than 250,000 instant pots were sold in the Canada and America only.

Most of the instant pots are sold on Amazon. More than 200,000 pieces were purchased on Amazon Prime Day 2016. In the kitchen category, the two models of the Instant Pot sit in the top 10 items of Amazon best sellers. All you need to do is to plug it in and tap the required button, and it does everything for you. It is user-friendly and gets meal done in no time. Local retail stores are the first option to buy the instant pot. However, you can buy it from an online store like Instant Pot Store and Amazon.

You can change your appearance and heal your illness through the low Carb diet. Whether you want to refill your energy, lose weight or reduce stress and diabetes, this book will help you achieve all that. In the next part, you will find some creative variety of recipes, which will result in the total transformation of your body if strictly adhere to. To make the book more comprehensive, we have introduced about 81 instant pot recipes categorized as low Carb delicious breakfast, lunch, dinner, soups, meat, vegetables and desserts. All the recipes included there will keep you healthy and reduce your sugar intake keeping diabetes and obesity at arms length.

CHAPTER 3: 81 LOW CARB INSTANT POT RECIPES

15 Tasty Breakfasts

1. Egg Muffins with Vegetables

Preparation Time: 3 Minutes
Yield: 2 Servings

Ingredients
1 tablespoon of Coconut oil
½ cup of baby Spinach
½ cup of carrots
1/3 cup of broccoli
Salt and black pepper, to taste
4 eggs
1-½ cup of water

Directions
Place a steamer basket in the instant pot and add about 1 to ½ cup of water.
Take a large bowl and whisk some eggs in it.
Then add the salt and pepper.
Next, add the carrots, broccoli, oil, and spinach.
Stir the ingredients properly.
Divide the mixture evenly between the silicone muffin cups.
Insert the silicone muffin cups in a steamer basket.
Cover the locking lid of the instant pot and adjust the high pressure and timer to 3 minutes.
When the instant pot timer beeps, turn it off.
After a minute, use a quick pressure release.
Open the lid of the pot and remove the muffins from the steamer basket.
Serve immediately.

Nutrition Facts
Servings: 2
Per Serving% Daily Value*
Calories 203
Total Fat 15.6g   20%
Saturated Fat 8.6g   43%
Trans Fat 0g
Cholesterol 327mg   119%
Sodium 153mg   7%
Potassium 296mg   6%
Total Carb 4.7g   2%
Dietary Fiber 1.3g   4%
Sugars 2.3g
Protein 11.9g
Vitamin A 194% · Vitamin C 29%
Calcium 5% · Iron 11%
*Based on a 2,000 calorie diet

2. Savory Breakfast Muffins

Preparation Time: 10 Minutes
Yield: 4 Servings

Dry Ingredients
½ cup of almond meal
4 tablespoons of hemp seed, raw
1 Oz. Parmesan cheese, finely-grated
1/3 cup of flax seed meal
1 tablespoon of yeast flakes
1/3 teaspoon of baking powder
1/4 teaspoon of salt

Wet Ingredients
4 eggs, beaten
1/3 cup of cottage cheese, reduced-fat
1/4 cup of green onion, thinly sliced

Directions

Place the steamer basket in the instant pot and add 2 cups of water.
Fine mist the silicon muffin cups with oil sprays.
Take an average sized bowl and mix the almond meal, hemp seed, flax seed, Parmesan cheese, yeast, and the baking powder.
Add the salt to give it some taste.
Using a separate bowl beat the eggs.
Then add the cottage cheese and green onions.
Properly mix the wet ingredients into the dry ingredients.
Fill the muffin cups with this mixture.
Insert the muffin cups in a steamer basket.
Cover the locking lid of the instant pot and adjust the high pressure for 10 minutes.
When the instant pot timer beeps, turn it off.
After a minute, use a quick pressure release.
Open the lid of the pot and remove the muffins from steamer basket.
Serve immediately.

Nutrition Facts

Servings: 4
Per Serving% Daily Value*
Calories 336
Total Fat 22g   28%
Saturated Fat 3.8g   19%
Trans Fat 0g
Cholesterol 170mg   62%
Sodium 663mg   29%
Potassium 590mg   13%
Total Carb 11.4g   4%
Dietary Fiber 6.2g   22%
Sugars 1.2g
Protein 23.8g
Vitamin A 11% · Vitamin C 2%
Calcium 13% · Iron 40%
*Based on a 2,000 calorie diet

3. Yummy Breakfast

Preparation Time: 10 Minutes
Yield: 2 Servings

Ingredients
1 large onion, diced
2 cups of chopped ham
2 cups of shredded cheddar cheese
10 large eggs
1/3 cup of almond milk
Salt and pepper to taste

Directions
Grease the instant pot with an oil spray.
Place the onions, ham, and cheese into the pot one after the other.
Using a bowl, combine the eggs, milk, salt, and pepper.
Pour the egg mixture over the ham and cheese in the pot.
Cover the locking lid of the instant pot and adjust the high pressure button for 10-12 minutes.
When the instant pot timer beeps, turn it off.
After a minute, use a quick pressure release.
Open the lid and serve immediately.

Nutrition Facts
Servings: 2
Per Serving % Daily Value*
Calories 1087
Total Fat 75.3g   97%
Saturated Fat 36.3g   181%
Trans Fat 0g
Cholesterol 1130mg   411%
Sodium 2831mg   123%
Potassium 1001mg   21%
Total Carb 17.4g   6%
Dietary Fiber 3.4g   12%
Sugars 7.8g
Protein 84.2g

Vitamin A 80% · Vitamin C 18%
Calcium 80% · Iron 38%
*Based on a 2,000 calorie diet

4. Boiled Egg for Breakfast

Preparation Time: 8 Minutes
Yield: 2 Servings

Ingredients
4 Pasture raised eggs
1 cup of water

Directions
The first step is to plug the instant pot and pour one cup of water in the bottom of the pot.
Place a steamer basket in the instant pot.
Put the eggs on top of the opened steamer basket.
Put the lid on.
Adjust the cooking time to 8 minutes on the display.
Close and lock the lid.
When the instant pot timer beeps, turn it off.
After a minute, use a quick pressure release.
Open the lid of the pot and remove the eggs.
Serve immediately.

Nutrition Facts
Servings: 2
Per Serving % Daily Value*
Calories 120
Total Fat 8g   10%
Saturated Fat 3g 15%
Trans Fat 0g
Cholesterol 358mg   130%

Sodium 144mg 6%
Potassium 1mg 0%
Total Carb 2g 1%
Dietary Fiber 0g 0%
Sugars 0g
Protein 12g
Vitamin A 20% · Vitamin C 4%
Calcium 3% · Iron 8%
*Based on a 2,000 calorie diet

5. Pressure Cooker Breakfast Quinoa

Preparation Time: 1 Minute
Yield: 2 Servings

Ingredients
2 cups of quinoa, uncooked
2 cups of water
2 tablespoons of stevia
1/3 teaspoon of vanilla extract or bean
1/3 teaspoon of cinnamon, ground
Pinch of salt, or to taste
1 cup of almond milk, optional

Directions
Add all the listed ingredients to the instant pot (excluding the almond milk).
Select the high pressure button and adjust the time to one minute.
When the instant pot timer becps, turn it off.
After a minute, use a quick pressure release.
Open the instant pot.
Serve it hot with almond milk if you prefer it that way.

Nutrition Facts
Servings: 2

Per Serving % Daily Value*
Calories 905
Total Fat 38.9g   50%
Saturated Fat 26.6g   133%
Trans Fat 0g
Cholesterol 0mg 0%
Sodium 112mg   5%
Potassium 1278mg   27%
Total Carb 16.2g 39%
Dietary Fiber 14.7g   53%
Sugars 4.1g
Protein 26.8g
Vitamin A 0% · Vitamin C 6%
Calcium 8% · Iron 54%
*Based on a 2,000 calorie diet

6. Delicious Pancake in Instant Pot

Preparation Time: 20-25 Minutes
Yield: 2 Servings

Ingredients
2 cups of almond meal
2 1/2 teaspoons of baking powder
2 tablespoons of stevia
2 large eggs
1 1/2 cups of almond milk

Directions
Whisk the eggs in a bowl and add all the listed ingredients.
Then, grease the interior of the instant pot with oil.
Pour in the mixture.
Seal the lid with the vent closed.
Then, adjust the instant pot to its manual mode.
Set the pressure to the lowest.
Adjust the cooking time to 20-25 minutes.
When the instant pot timer beeps, turn it off.

After a minute, use a quick pressure release.
Open the instant pot.
Using a spatula, scrape off the cake from the sides of the pot.
Serve with your favorite toppings.

Nutrition Facts
Servings: 2
Per Serving % Daily Value*
Calories 1041
Total Fat 95.4g   122%
Saturated Fat 43.2g   216%
Trans Fat 0g
Cholesterol 186mg   68%
Sodium 104mg   5%
Potassium 1868mg   40%
Total Carb 33.7g   11%
Dietary Fiber 16g 57%
Sugars 10.4g
Protein 30.5g
Vitamin A 8% · Vitamin C 8%
Calcium 45% · Iron 44%
*Based on a 2,000 calorie diet

7. Eggs and Bacon Cups

Preparation Time: 10 Minutes
Yield: 4 Servings

Ingredients
8 organic eggs
10 slices of bacon
2 Oz. Cheese
Salt and black pepper, to taste

Directions

Place a steamer basket in the instant pot and add ½ to 1 cup of water.
Take a silicon muffin cup and line it with bacon strips.
Crack one egg into each hole and sprinkle the cheese, salt, and pepper.
Insert the muffin cup in a steamer basket.
Cover the locking lid of the instant pot and adjust the high pressure to 10 minutes.
When the instant pot timer beeps, turn it off.
After a minute, use a quick pressure release.
Open the lid of the pot and remove the muffins from steamer basket.
Serve immediately.

Nutrition Facts
Servings: 4
Per Serving % Daily Value*
Calories 440
Total Fat 33.3g   43%
Saturated Fat 12.3g   61%
Trans Fat 0g
Cholesterol 394mg   143%
Sodium 1308mg 57%
Potassium 401mg   9%
Total Carb 1.6g   1%
Dietary Fiber 0g 0%
Sugars 0.8g
Protein 32.2g
Vitamin A 20% · Vitamin C 0%
Calcium 12% · Iron 13%
*Based on a 2,000 calorie diet

8. Avocado Bread

Preparation Time: 25 Minutes
Yield: 4 Servings

Ingredients
3 cups of almond flour
2 teaspoons of baking soda

1/3 teaspoon of salt
1 cup of avocado, mashed
4 tablespoons of coconut oil, melted
1 teaspoon of vanilla extract
2 tablespoons of stevia
2 small eggs, room temperature
1 cup chopped walnuts

Directions

Grease a small size push pan with an oil spray.
Mix the almond flour, salt and baking soda in a large bowl.
Using a blender, mix the walnuts and avocados until it gets creamy.
Then add the coconut oil, stevia, vanilla, and eggs in the processor.
Beat until it is properly mixed.
Combine the wet ingredients with the dry ones.
Pour this batter into the pan.
Place the trivet on the bottom of the instant pot.
Add 2 cups of water.
Make a sling of aluminum foil.
Place it on the trivet.
Then place the pan on top.
Close and lock the instant pot and cook it using a high pressure for 25 minutes.
Thereafter set a10 minutes natural release.
Open the pot and serve the bread.

Nutrition Facts

Servings: 4
Per Serving % Daily Value*
Calories 540
Total Fat 51g   65%
Saturated Fat 15.6g   78%
Trans Fat 0g
Cholesterol 69mg   25%
Sodium 859mg   37%
Potassium 367mg   8%
Total Carb 11g   4%
Dietary Fiber 6.8g   24%

Sugars 0.8g
Protein 15g
Vitamin A 5% · Vitamin C 7%
Calcium 3% · Iron 9%
*Based on a 2,000 calorie diet

9. Scramble Egg in Instant Pot

Preparation Time: 7 Minutes
Yield: 2 Servings

Ingredients
2 eggs
1 tablespoon of almond milk
½ tablespoon of butter
Salt and pepper

Directions
Using an oil spray, grease the heat proof bowl.
Break the eggs into the bowl.
Then add the milk, salt, and pepper.
Beat the eggs until it gets even.
Put one cup of water in the Instant pot.
Then add the trivet.
Set the bowl on the top of the trivet.
Close the pot and its steam vent.
Set the pot to a low pressure for 7 minutes.
Release pressure immediately after the timer is down.
Release the steam.
Stir the eggs with a fork to see if they are cooked properly.
Serve right away.

Nutrition Facts
Servings: 2
Per Serving % Daily Value*

Calories 106
Total Fat 9g   12%
Saturated Fat 4.8g   24%
Trans Fat 0g
Cholesterol 171mg   62%
Sodium 83mg   4%
Potassium 80mg 2%
Total Carb 0.8g   0%
Dietary Fiber 0.2g   1%
Sugars 0.6g
Protein 5.8g
Vitamin A 10% · Vitamin C 0%
Calcium 2% · Iron 5%
*Based on a 2,000 calorie diet

10. Instant Pot Berries and Cream Breakfast Cake

Preparation Time: 25 Minutes
Yield: 4 Servings

Ingredients
6 organic eggs
4 scoops stevia
2 tablespoons of butter, melted
3/4 cup of ricotta Cheese
3/4 cup of plain yogurt
1 teaspoon of vanilla extract
1 cup of whole almond flour
Pinch of salt
2 teaspoons of baking powder
1/3 cup of Berry Compote

Glaze Ingredients
1/4 cup yogurt
1/2 teaspoon vanilla extract

1 teaspoon almond milk

Directions
First, generously grease a 6 cup Bundt cake pan with a cooking spray.
Using a bowl, whisk the eggs with the stevia.
Then add the butter, cheese, yogurt, and vanilla.
Mix until it is smooth.
Use a separate bowl; mix the flour, salt, and baking powder together.
Pour the egg mixture in it.
Then pour this mixture into the prepared Bundt pan.
Drop Berry Compote in tablespoons on top of the prepared batter and swirl it in with a knife.
Add 2 cups of water to the instant pot and place a trivet inside it.
Thereafter place the Bundt pan on the top of the trivet.
Cook it at high pressure for 25 minutes.
Meanwhile, while doing that prepare the glaze by mixing all the glaze ingredients and set it aside.
Once the timer beeps, use a natural release for 10 minutes and then release the pressure.
Remove the cake pan from the instant cooker.
Scrape off the sides and gently turn the cake over onto a flat plate.
Sprinkle it with Sweet Yogurt Glaze.
Serve.

Nutrition Facts
Servings: 4
Per Serving % Daily Value*
Calories 357
Total Fat 23.3g   30%
Saturated Fat 10.5g   53%
Trans Fat 0g
Cholesterol 278mg   101%
Sodium 299mg   13%
Potassium 513mg   11%
Total Carb 7.5g   6%
Dietary Fiber 1.3g   5%
Sugars 8.7g
Protein 18.5g

Vitamin A 23% · Vitamin C 1%
Calcium 27% · Iron 9%
*Based on a 2,000 calorie diet

11. Easy Two Ingredients Jam in Instant Pot

Preparation Time: 2 Minutes
Yield: 8 Servings

Ingredients
2 pounds of blueberries, fresh or frozen
1 pound of stevia

Directions
Add both ingredients to the pot and reduce the heat on the pot to a low pressure.
Turn the Sauté function on the Instant Pot until the mixture boils.
There will be bubbles all around the blueberries.
When it boils, put on the lid.
If using an electric cooker set it to a high pressure for 2 minutes.
Once the timer beeps, use a natural release for 10 minutes and then release the pressure.
Pour the jam into the clean glass jars.
Store in the refrigerator or serve.

Nutrition Facts
Servings: 8
Per Serving % Daily Value*
Calories 58
Total Fat 0.8g   1%
Saturated Fat 0g 0%
Trans Fat 0g
Cholesterol 0mg 0%
Sodium 0mg   0%
Potassium 67mg   1%
Total Carb 14.2g 5%
Dietary Fiber 3.3g   12%

Sugars 10g
Protein 0.8g
Vitamin A 0% · Vitamin C 5%
Calcium 0% · Iron 0%
*Based on a 2,000 calorie diet

12. Breakfast Cobbler

Preparation Time: 15 Minutes
Yield: 4 Servings

Ingredients
1 pear, diced
2 apples, diced
2 plums, diced
2 scoops stevia
3 tablespoons of coconut oil
½ teaspoon of ground cinnamon
1/3 cup coconut, unsweetened and shredded
1/3 cup pecan, pieces
2 tablespoons of sunflower seeds
1 cup Coconut cream, for garnishing

Directions
Place all the fruits in the instant pot.
Add the stevia and sprinkle the cinnamon on top of it.
Guard the lid of the instant Pot and close off the pressure valve.
Adjust the Steam button to 10 minutes.
Let the fruits cook properly.
Afterwards, open the pot and remove the lid.
Transfer the cooked fruit into a serving bowl.
 Now place the coconut, oil, pecans, and sunflower seeds into the same pot liquid and press the Sauté button.
Let the content, steam.
Remember to stir it from time to time.
Let it cook for an additional 5 minutes.
Remove it and then garnish it with the fruits.
Serve with coconut whip cream.

Nutrition Facts
Servings: 4
Per Serving % Daily Value*
Calories 575
Total Fat 50.7g   65%
Saturated Fat 25.8g   129%
Trans Fat 0g
Cholesterol 0mg 0%
Sodium 12mg   1%
Potassium 536mg   11%
Total Carb 34.1g 11%
Dietary Fiber 9.9g   35%
Sugars 22.1g
Protein 6g
Vitamin A 4% · Vitamin C 26%
Calcium 3% · Iron 19%
*Based on a 2,000 calorie diet

13. Breakfast Porridge

Preparation 3 Minutes
Yield: 2 Servings

Ingredients
½ cup Cashews, raw
1/3 cup Pecan
1/2 cup Coconut, Unsweetened, dry and shredded
1 cup Water
2 tablespoons of Coconut Oil, melted
2 scoops stevia

Directions
Mix all of the ingredients excluding water, coconut oil, and stevia in a blender and blend for around 30 seconds.
Transfer the contents to the bowl of your Instant Pot.
Add the stevia, water, oil.

Close the pot and press the Porridge button.
Once the display read 3 minutes allow it to cook.
After 3 minutes release the pressure valve and remove the lid.
Stir the porridge and serve with fresh fruits.

Nutrition Facts
Servings: 2
Per Serving % Daily Value*
Calories 580
Total Fat 56.2g   72%
Saturated Fat 22.8g   114%
Trans Fat 0g
Cholesterol 0mg 0%
Sodium 13mg   1%
Potassium 382mg   8%
Total Carb 18.2g 6%
Dietary Fiber 5.8g   21%
Sugars 4g
Protein 8.9g
Vitamin A 1% · Vitamin C 3%
Calcium 3% · Iron 31%
*Based on a 2,000 calorie diet

14. Simple and Delicious Muffin Recipes

Preparation Time: 10 Minutes
Yield: 4 Servings

Ingredients
4 organic eggs, beaten
1/4 teaspoon lemon pepper seasoning
4 tablespoons Jack cheese
2 large white onions, chopped
2 Oz. cooked bacon strips, crumbled

Directions
Take a steamer basket and place it in the instant pot and then pour a

reasonable amount of water into it.
Take a bowl and whisk the eggs into it.
Then add the lemon pepper seasoning.
Whisk to combine properly.
Divide the jack cheese, white onions and precooked bacon between the 4 to 6 silicone muffin cups.
Divide the whisked eggs into the muffin cups.
Stir with a fork.
Line the muffin cups in a basket inside an instant pot.
Cover and then set the timer to 7 minutes.
When the timer beeps, turn it off.
Then perform a quick pressure release.
Open the lid.
Remove muffins from steamer basket.
Serve and enjoy.

Nutrition Facts
Servings: 4
Per Serving % Daily Value*
Calories 217
Total Fat 16.3g   21%
Saturated Fat 7.1g   35%
Trans Fat 0g
Cholesterol 198mg   72%
Sodium 525mg   23%
Potassium 161mg 3%
Total Carb 1.2g   0%
Dietary Fiber 0.2g   1%
Sugars 0.5g
Protein 16.9g
Vitamin A 20% · Vitamin C 2%
Calcium 14% · Iron 6%
*Based on a 2,000 caloric diet

15. Instant Pot Bacon Ranch Potatoes

Preparation Time: 7 Minutes

Yield: 4 Servings

Ingredients
2 pounds of red potatoes, scrubbed and cut into pieces
1 cup of bacon strips, cubed
2 tablespoons of water
3 teaspoons of dried parsley
1 teaspoon of salt
2 teaspoons of garlic powder
4 Oz. Cheddar cheese, shredded
1/2 cup of the Ranch dressing

Directions
Take an instant pot and add the bacon, potatoes, and water into it.
Add the salt, dried parsley, and garlic powder
Set the timer of instant pot to 7 minutes.
Release the pressure and open the lid.
Add the cheese and ranch dressing.
Stir to mix properly.
 Serve immediately.

Nutrition Facts
Servings: 4
Per Serving % Daily Value*
Calories 460
Total Fat 23.2g   30%
Saturated Fat 10.5g   52%
Trans Fat 0g
Cholesterol 65mg   24%
Sodium 1680mg 73%
Potassium 1261mg   27%
Total Carb 39.6g 13%
Dietary Fiber 4.1g   15%
Sugars 3.6g
Protein 23.9g
Vitamin A 25% · Vitamin C 37%
Calcium 18% · Iron 14%
*Based on a 2,000 calorie diet

16 Mouth-Watering Soups

1. Instant Pot Squash Soup

Preparation Time: 20 Minutes
Yield: 6 Servings

Ingredients
7 cups of chicken broth
3 ounces of diced tomatoes
6 ounces of green beans
2 cups of butternut squash, peeled and seeded
1 cup of zucchini, sliced
1 cup of onion, chopped
2 cloves of garlic, minced
4 teaspoons of Worcestershire sauce
3 teaspoons of dried rosemary leaves
Salt and black pepper, to taste
4 tablespoons of coconut oil

Directions
With your electric instant pot, press the sauté button.
Once the instant pot gets hot, add the oil, onion, pepper, salt, and garlic
Next, add all the remaining listed ingredients.
Close the instant pot and set timer to 20 minutes
After 20 minutes, let the pressure release by itself.
Serve the soup into a bowl and enjoy.

Nutrition Facts
Servings: 6
Per Serving % Daily Value*
Calories 173
Total Fat 10.9g   14%
Saturated Fat 8.4g   42%
Trans Fat 0g
Cholesterol 0mg 0%

Sodium 934mg   41%
Potassium 585mg   12%
Total Carb 12.9g 4%
Dietary Fiber 3g 11%
Sugars 4.4g
Protein 7.3g
Vitamin A 178% · Vitamin C 36%
Calcium 5% · Iron 9%
*Based on a 2,000 calorie diet

2. Mushroom Soup

Preparation Time: 20 Minutes
Yield: 4 Servings

Ingredients
6 cups vegetable broth
2 medium onions, chopped
3 cups celery, sliced
½ cup baby carrots
½ cup pearl barley
14 Oz. Dried mushrooms, chopped
1 cup peas, thawed
Salt and white pepper, to taste
⅓ cup sour cream

Directions
Combine all the ingredients, except for the sour cream, in an instant pot.
Close the instant pot and set timer to 20 minutes.
After 20 minutes, let the pressure release by itself.
Serve the soup in a bowl and garnish it the soup with sour cream.
Enjoy.

Nutrition Facts
Servings: 4
Per Serving % Daily Value*
Calories 275
Total Fat 7g   9%

Saturated Fat 3.2g   16%
Trans Fat 0g
Cholesterol 8mg 3%
Sodium 1236mg 54%
Potassium 1114mg   24%
Total Carb 38.4g 13%
Dietary Fiber 9.4g   34%
Sugars 8.9g
Protein 16.6g
Vitamin A 74% · Vitamin C 40%
Calcium 8% · Iron 29%
*Based on a 2,000 calorie diet

3. Spinach Soup

Preparation Time: 20 Minutes
Yield: 4 Servings

Ingredients
6 cups vegetable broth
1 cup tomatoes, un-drained
½ cup dried brown lentils
1 cup chopped onions
¼ cup celery, carrot
3 large cloves garlic, minced
2 teaspoons curry powder
½ teaspoon chili powder
2 cups chopped spinach, thawed and drained
Salt and pepper, to taste

Directions
Combine all the ingredients in an instant pot
Set the timer to 20 minutes.
After 20 minutes, let the pressure release by itself.
Serve.

Nutrition Facts
Servings: 4

Per Serving % Daily Value*
Calories 138
Total Fat 2.6g   3%
Saturated Fat 0.6g   3%
Trans Fat 0g
Cholesterol 0mg 0%
Sodium 1169mg   51%
Potassium 589mg   13%
Total Carb 15.9g 5%
Dietary Fiber 3.5g   13%
Sugars 3.7g
Protein 12.3g
Vitamin A 64% · Vitamin C 23%
Calcium 4% · Iron 10%
*Based on a 2,000 calorie diet

4. Spicy Barley Soup

Preparation Time: 20 Minutes
Yield: 4 Servings

Ingredients
2 quarts of vegetable broth
1-1/2 cup of onions, chopped
½ cup of sliced mushrooms
½ cup of carrot
½ cup of celery
½ cup of turnip
1 large clove of garlic, minced
3 tablespoons of tomato paste
¼ cup of pearl barley
2 bay leaves
1 teaspoon of dried marjoram leaves
½ teaspoon of thyme leaves
Salt and pepper, to taste

Directions

Put all the ingredients in an instant pot.
Close the instant pot and set timer to 20 minutes.
After 20 minutes, let the pressure release by itself.
Serve.

Nutrition Facts
Servings: 4
Per Serving % Daily Value*
Calories 161
Total Fat 3.2g   4%
Saturated Fat 0.8g   4%
Trans Fat 0g
Cholesterol 0mg   0%
Sodium 1572mg   68%
Potassium 759mg   16%
Total Carb 20.7g 7%
Dietary Fiber 4.4g   16%
Sugars 5.8g
Protein 12.6g
Vitamin A 87% · Vitamin C 17%
Calcium 5% · Iron 16%
*Based on a 2,000 calorie diet

5. Vegetable Soup

Preparation Time: 20 Minutes
Yield: 4 Servings

Ingredients
7 cups of chicken broth
½ cup of dry red wine
1 pound of chicken breast, cubed and boneless
15 Oz. of Chickpea, rinsed, drained
4 cups of cabbage, coarsely shredded
1 cup of onion, chopped
1 cup of leek, chopped
½ cup of turnip

½ cup of carrots
1 green bell pepper
4 cloves garlic, chopped
1 teaspoon of dried thyme leaves
Salt and pepper, to taste

Directions
Mix all the ingredients in an instant pot.
Adjust the timer to 20 minutes.
After 20 minutes, let the pressure release by itself.
Serve into a soup bowl and enjoy.

Nutrition Facts
Servings: 4
Per Serving% Daily Value*
Calories 675
Total Fat 12g   15%
Saturated Fat 1.4g   7%
Trans Fat 0g
Cholesterol 73mg 26%
Sodium 1460mg 63%
Potassium 2087mg   44%
Total Carb 82.6g 28%
Dietary Fiber 22.5g   80%
Sugars 20g
Protein 55.4g
Vitamin A 128% · Vitamin C 165%
Calcium 16% · Iron 53%
*Based on a 2,000 calorie diet

6. Spicy Chicken Soup

Preparation Time: 25 Minutes
Yield: 3 Servings

Ingredients
2 quarts of Chicken Stock

14 OZ of stewed tomatoes,
1 pound of boneless, skinless chicken breast, cubed
3 cups of onions, coarsely chopped
1 cup of celery
1/3 cup of almond meal
Handful of Thyme leaves
1/6 teaspoon of ground cloves
Salt and pepper, to taste

Directions
Combine all the ingredients in an instant pot.
Adjust the time to 25minutes.
After 25 minutes, let the pressure release by itself.
Serve it in a soup bowl and enjoy.

Nutrition Facts
Servings: 3
Per Serving% Daily Value*
Calories 319
Total Fat 5.9g 8%
Saturated Fat 0.5g 2%
Trans Fat 0g
Cholesterol 97mg 35%
Sodium 2151mg 94%
Potassium 1028mg 22%
Total Carb 29.1g 10%
Dietary Fiber 7g 25%
Sugars 8.3g
Protein 37.9g
Vitamin A 18% · Vitamin C 29%
Calcium 9% · Iron 12%
*Based on a 2,000 calorie diet

7. Oriental Soup with Noodles and Chicken

Preparation Time: 30 Minutes
Yield: 6 Servings

Ingredients
1 Oz. Shiitake mushrooms
2 cups Hot water
16 Oz. Chicken broth
2 tablespoons of dry sherry
8 ounces of boneless chicken breast, cubed
½ cup of white mushrooms
½ cup of carrots
2 teaspoons of light soy sauce
1 teaspoon of five-spice powder
4 OZ. Snow peas, trimmed
3 cups of dried chow Mein noodles
Salt and pepper, to taste

Directions
Take a bowl and add the dried mushrooms, let it sit for 15 minutes, thereafter drain the water out and slice the mushrooms. Remember to discard any rough parts.
Combine the mushrooms and the remaining ingredients except for the snow peas, Chow Mein noodles, in the instant pot.
Cover and adjust the timer to 15 minutes.
After 15 minutes, let the pressure release by itself.
Then open the pot, add the snow peas and the chow Mein noodles.
Now cover the pot and set the timer to 10 minutes at a low pressure.
Open the pot after it releases the steam by itself.
Serve the soup into a bowl and enjoy.

Nutrition Facts
Nutrition Facts
Servings: 6
Per Serving % Daily Value*
Calories 225
Total Fat 10.2g   13%

Saturated Fat 1.9g   9%
Trans Fat 0g
Cholesterol 34mg   12%
Sodium 612mg   27%
Potassium 284mg   6%
Total Carb 17.3g   6%
Dietary Fiber 2.4g   8%
Sugars 2.2g
Protein 15.7g
Vitamin A 58% · Vitamin C 16%
Calcium 2% · Iron 13%
*Based on a 2,000 calorie diet

8. Lamb Soup with Barley

Preparation Time: 25 Minutes
Yield: 6 Servings

Ingredients
2 quarts of Chicken Stock
1 pounds of lean lamb stew meat, cubed
2-quart of water
2 cups of onions, chopped
2 cups of carrots, chopped
2 cups of turnips, chopped
1 cup of sliced celery
1 tablespoon of garlic, minced
1 teaspoon of rosemary leaves
2 bays of Leafs
Salt and pepper, to taste

Directions
Mix all the ingredients in an instant pot.
Adjust the timer to 25minutes at a high pressure.
After 25 minutes, let the pressure release by itself.
Serve in a soup bowl and enjoy.

Nutrition Facts

Servings: 6
Per Serving % Daily Value*
Calories 218
Total Fat 7.2g 9%
Saturated Fat 2.6g 13%
Trans Fat 0g
Cholesterol 38mg 14%
Sodium 1556mg 68%
Potassium 478mg 10%
Total Carb 23.8g 8%
Dietary Fiber 5.5g 20%
Sugars 11.6g
Protein 13.9g
Vitamin A 284% · Vitamin C 55%
Calcium 9% · Iron 11%
*Based on a 2,000 calorie diet

9. Buffalo Chicken Soup

Preparation Time: 15 Minutes
Yield: 6 Servings

Ingredients

2 pounds of Boneless Skinless Chicken Breasts
10 cups of chicken bone broth
1/3 cup of diced Celery
½ cup of diced onion
2 cloves of garlic, chopped
½ tablespoon of ranch dressing mix
2 tablespoons of butter
1/3 cup of hot sauce
1 cup of cheddar cheese, shredded
1 cup of heavy cream

Directions

Mix all the ingredients in the instant pot except for the heavy cream and cheese.
Pressurize it for 15 minutes and quickly depressurize after that.
Carefully remove the chicken from pot.
Shred the chicken and then return it to the soup.
Add the heavy cream and cheese once done.
Stir and then serve it in a bowl.
Enjoy.

Nutrition Facts
Servings: 6
Per Serving % Daily Value*
Calories 530
Total Fat 28.8g   37%
Saturated Fat 14.1g   71%
Trans Fat 0g
Cholesterol 192mg   70%
Sodium 1216mg   53%
Potassium 453mg   10%
Total Carb 2.5g   1%
Dietary Fiber 0.4g   1%
Sugars 0.8g
Protein 61.7g
Vitamin A 25% · Vitamin C 18%
Calcium 14% · Iron 12%
*Based on a 2,000 calorie diet

10. Carrot Soup

Preparation Time: 15 Minutes
Yield: 6 Servings

Ingredient
10 large carrots, peeled and chopped
2 onions, chopped

2 cloves of garlic, peeled
15 Oz Coconut milk
1 cup of broth
1/3 of cup peanut butter
1 tablespoon of red curry paste
Salt, to taste

Directions
Mix all the ingredients in an instant pot.
Adjust the timer to 15 minutes.
After 15 minutes, let the pressure release by itself.
Serve it in a soup bowl and enjoy.

Nutrition Facts
Servings: 6
Per Serving % Daily Value*
Calories 329
Total Fat 25.1g 32%
Saturated Fat 16.8g 84%
Trans Fat 0g
Cholesterol 0mg 0%
Sodium 445mg 19%
Potassium 755mg 16%
Total Carb 23g 8%
Dietary Fiber 6.2g 22%
Sugars 11.3g
Protein 7.5g
Vitamin A 668% · Vitamin C 20%
Calcium 5% · Iron 18%
*Based on a 2,000 calorie diet

11. Instant Pot Broccoli Cheddar Soup

Preparation Time: 10 Minutes
Yield: 4 Servings

Ingredients
5 cups of broccoli florets
1 onion, chopped
6 cups of chicken bone broth
3 carrots, chopped
1 tablespoon of garlic
Salt, to taste
2 cups of grated cheddar cheese
½ cup of heavy cream
1 tablespoon of olive oil

Directions
Add the olive oil into an instant pot and turn the "sauté" setting.
When it gets hot start adding the onion until it becomes translucent.
Press the off button thereafter.
Open the instant pot and add all the remaining ingredients except for the cheese.
Close the pot and adjust the manual mode to 5 minutes.
After 5 minutes, let the steam release by itself.
Then serve soup it in a bowl with cheese on top.
Enjoy.

Nutrition Facts
Servings: 4
Per Serving% Daily Value*
Calories 423
Total Fat 28.2g   36%
Saturated Fat 15.9g   79%
Trans Fat 0g
Cholesterol 80mg   29%
Sodium 903mg   39%
Potassium 621mg   13%
Total Carb 16.5g 5%

Dietary Fiber 4.7g   17%
Sugars 5.7g
Protein 27.8g
Vitamin A 305% · Vitamin C 178%
Calcium 38% · Iron 8%
*Based on a 2,000 calorie diet

12. Vidalia onion Soup

Preparation Time: 15 Minutes
Yield: 4 Servings

Ingredients
6 cups of chicken broth
6 cups of Vidalia onions
2 cloves of garlic, minced
1 teaspoon of stevia
1teaspoons of sage leaves, dried
1 bay leaf
Salt and white pepper, to taste
2 tablespoons of Corn starch
4 tablespoons of Water
Chives, garnishing

Directions
Mix all the ingredients, except for the cornstarch and water in an instant pot.
Cook it using a high pressure for 10 minutes.
Pour in the combined cornstarch and water, and stir it for 2 to 3 minutes.
Process the soup in the blender until it is smooth.
Season it to give it some taste and serve with chives.

Nutrition Facts
Servings: 4
Per Serving % Daily Value*
Calories 148
Total Fat 2.3g   3%
Saturated Fat 0.6g   3%

Trans Fat 0g
Cholesterol 0mg 0%
Sodium 1152mg   50%
Potassium 571mg 12%
Total Carb 22.7g 8%
Dietary Fiber 3.9g   14%
Sugars 8.4g
Protein 9.3g
Vitamin A 1% · Vitamin C 21%
Calcium 5% · Iron 7%
*Based on a 2,000 calorie diet

13. Dilled Carrot Soup

Preparation Time: 15 Minutes
Yield: 4 Servings

Ingredients
3 cups of chicken broth
1 cup of tomatoes
1.5 of pound carrots, sliced
2 cups of onions
1 potato, peeled, cubed
2 garlic cloves, minced
1 teaspoon of dill weed
4 tablespoons of lemon juice
Salt and black pepper, to taste
6 tablespoons of plain yogurt

Directions
Mix all the ingredients, except for the lemon juice, and yogurt in instant pot; cover and cook using a high pressure heat for 15 minutes.
Process the soup in a blender to gain some level of smoothness consistently.
Sprinkle the lemon juice over the top.
Serve with the dollop of yogurt.

Nutrition Facts

Servings: 4
Per Serving % Daily Value*
Calories 185
Total Fat 1.6g   2%
Saturated Fat 0.7g   3%
Trans Fat 0g
Cholesterol 1mg   1%
Sodium 716mg   31%
Potassium 1155mg   25%
Total Carb 34.6g   12%
Dietary Fiber 7g   25%
Sugars 14.8g
Protein 8.5g
Vitamin A 961% · Vitamin C 61%
Calcium 10% · Iron 9%
*Based on a 2,000 calorie diet

14. Garlic Soup

Preparation Time: 15 Minutes
Yield: 4 Servings

Ingredients
1 quart chicken broth
6 cloves of garlic, finely chopped
1 teaspoon of cumin
1 teaspoon of oregano leaves, dried
Salt, to taste
Cayenne pepper, to taste
Chopped cilantro, as garnish

Directions
Mix all the listed ingredients in an instant pot; cover and cook using a high pressure for 15 minutes.
Let it release the steam by itself.
Serve.

Nutrition Facts
Servings: 4
Per Serving % Daily Value*
Calories 50
Total Fat 1.6g 2%
Saturated Fat 0.4g 2%
Trans Fat 0g
Cholesterol 0mg 0%
Sodium 806mg 35%
Potassium 268mg 6%
Total Carb 3.1g 1%
Dietary Fiber 0.5g 2%
Sugars 0.8g
Protein 5.4g
Vitamin A 13% · Vitamin C 5%
Calcium 2% · Iron 7%
*Based on a 2,000 calorie diet

15. Split-Pea Soup with Ham

Preparation Time: 15 Minutes
Yield: 8 Servings

Ingredients
1½ quarts water
14 Oz. chicken broth
1 pound of split peas
1½ cups of lean ham
1 cup of chopped carrots
1 teaspoon of dried marjoram leaves
Salt and pepper, to taste

Directions
Mix all the listed ingredients in an instant pot; cover it and cook using a high pressure for 20 minutes.
Let the steam release by itself.
Serve.

Nutrition Facts
Servings: 8
Per Serving % Daily Value*
Calories 306
Total Fat 3.4g 4%
Saturated Fat 0.8g 4%
Trans Fat 0g
Cholesterol 42mg 15%
Sodium 1179mg 51%
Potassium 1253mg 27%
Total Carb 36.5g 12%
Dietary Fiber 14.8g 53%
Sugars 5.4g
Protein 32.5g
Vitamin A 80% · Vitamin C 3%
Calcium 5% · Iron 19%
*Based on a 2,000 calorie diet

16. Down-Home Soup

Preparation Time: 20 Minutes
Yield: 8-12 Servings

Ingredients
2 quarts chicken broth
1/2 cup of black-eyed peas
1/4 cup of pearl barley
4 pack of ham hocks
1 cup of green beans cut
1 cup of onion, chopped
1/4 cup of carrot, chopped
1 clove of garlic, minced
2 teaspoon of s basil leaves
1 bay leaf
1 cup of tomatoes, cubed
Salt and pepper, to taste

Directions

Mix all the listed ingredients in an instant pot; cover it and cook using a high pressure for 20 minutes.
Let it release the steam by itself.
Remove the bay leaves and serve.

Nutrition Facts

Servings: 8
Per Serving % Daily Value*
Calories 129
Total Fat 3.2g   4%
Saturated Fat 0.9g   5%
Trans Fat 0g
Cholesterol 22mg   8%
Sodium 1043mg   45%
Potassium 504mg   11%
Total Carb 11.5g   4%
Dietary Fiber 2.6g   9%
Sugars 2.3g
Protein 13.8g
Vitamin A 30% · Vitamin C 11%
Calcium 2% · Iron 9%
*Based on a 2,000 calorie diet

10 Vegetable Recipes

1. Veggies Risotto

Preparation Time: 25 Minutes
Yield: 4 Servings

Ingredients
1 onion, diced
4 tablespoons of olive oil
1 fennel, diced
1/3 asparagus, diced
Salt, to taste
2 garlic cloves
⅓ Cup of wine
½ lemon, zest
4 cups of vegetable soup or stock
2 tablespoons of organic butter
1 cup of Parmesan cheese, grated

Ingredients to top the risotto
2 tablespoons of oil
½ fennels
½ asparagus, cubed
1/3 teaspoon of salt
½ lemon, juice

Directions
Press the sauté button on the Instant Pot and cook the onions for 4-6 minutes in the oil.
Add the fennel and asparagus.
Thereafter, add all the remaining listed ingredients as well (excluding butter and cheese)
Close the lid of instant pot.
Adjust to the manual mode with a High pressure set to 7 minutes.
Meanwhile at the same time, heat the olive oil in the pan and add all the topping ingredients.

Cook for about 10 minutes.
Once the timer goes off, let the steam release by itself.
Open the lid and pour in the butter and cheese.
Serve it with pan ingredients as the topping.

Nutrition Facts
Servings: 4
Per Serving% Daily Value*
Calories 339
Total Fat 26.3g 34%
Saturated Fat 9.7g 49%
Trans Fat 0g
Cholesterol 35mg 13%
Sodium 455mg 20%
Potassium 588mg 13%
Total Carb 15.2g 5%
Dietary Fiber 5.1g 18%
Sugars 2.6g
Protein 11.6g
Vitamin A 19% · Vitamin C 43%
Calcium 25% · Iron 7%
*Based on a 2,000 calorie diet

2. Coconut Cabbage in Instant Pot

Preparation Time: 10 Minutes
Yield: 4 Servings

Ingredients
2 tablespoons of coconut oil
1 brown onion, halved and sliced
1 teaspoon of salt
1 large clove of garlic, diced
1 red chili, sliced
1 tablespoon of mustard seeds
1 tablespoon of curry powder
2 tablespoons of turmeric powder

2 cups of cabbage, quartered and shredded or sliced (core removed)
1 cup of carrot, peeled and sliced
2 tablespoons of lemon juice
½ cup of unsweetened coconut
2 tablespoons of olive oil
⅓ Cup of water

Directions
Press the Sauté function on instant Pot and cook the onions in the oil for 5 minutes
Then add the entire reaming listed ingredient one after the other.
Press the Keep Warm button.
Then lock the lid and set time to 5 minutes.
Afterwards, use the quick release to let the steam escape.
Serve.

Nutrition Facts
Servings: 4
Per Serving% Daily Value*
Calories 221
Total Fat 18.7g   24%
Saturated Fat 10.1g   51%
Trans Fat 0g
Cholesterol 0mg 0%
Sodium 616mg   27%
Potassium 384mg   8%
Total Carb 14g   5%
Dietary Fiber 5g   18%
Sugars 5.1g
Protein 2.7g
Vitamin A 156% · Vitamin C 42%
Calcium 5% · Iron 22%
*Based on a 2,000 calorie diet

3. Zucchini Casserole

Yield: 6 Servings
Preparation Time: 20 Minutes
Ingredients
2 slices of red onions
2 green bell peppers cut into thin strips
6 big slices of zucchini
1 cup of diced tomatoes
Salt
A grounded black pepper
4 tablespoons of butter
And a ½ cup of grated Parmesan cheese

Directions
Mix all the listed ingredients (excluding butter and the Parmesan cheese) in an instant pot and cook for about 20 minutes.
After 20 minutes open the pot and add the butter with the cheese.
Stir for 3 minutes.
Then serve.

Nutrition Facts
Servings: 6
Per Serving% Daily Value*
Calories 212
Total Fat 12.5g   16%
Saturated Fat 7.7g   38%
Trans Fat 0g
Cholesterol 34mg   12%
Sodium 291mg   13%
Potassium 1048mg   22%
Total Carb 19.1g   6%
Dietary Fiber 5.2g   19%
Sugars 9.9g
Protein 11.1g
Vitamin A 86% · Vitamin C 231%
Calcium 18% · Iron 8%
*Based on a 2,000 calorie diet

4. Simple Slow Cook Recipe

Yield: 6 Servings
Preparation Time: 20 Minutes

Ingredients
1 cup of carrot
1 cup of corn
1 cup of turnip
1 can cream of mushroom soup
Salt
Parsley, for garnishing
Pepper
And a 1/3 tablespoon of garlic powder

Directions
Place all the ingredients in an instant pot.
Cover and set the timer to 20 minutes.
Afterwards, use the quick release button to let the steam out.
Serve.

Nutrition Facts
Servings: 6
Per Serving% Daily Value*
Calories 82
Total Fat 3.3g   4%
Saturated Fat 0.7g   4%
Trans Fat 0g
Cholesterol 0mg 0%
Sodium 378mg   16%
Potassium 260mg   6%
Total Carb 12.3g 4%
Dietary Fiber 1.9g   7%
Sugars 3.5g
Protein 2.3g
Vitamin A 131% · Vitamin C 34%
Calcium 3% · Iron 11%
*Based on a 2,000 calorie diet

5. Sweet and Sour Beet Roots

Yield: 6 Servings
Preparation Time: 12 Hours

Ingredients
1 cup of stevia
4 tablespoons of almond flour
1/3 cup of water
2/4 cup of white vinegar
And 4 cans of already drained whole beets

Directions
Use a bowl, mix the stevia and flour with the vinegar and water.
Once the liquid is formed, empty it in an instant pot.
Thereafter, add the beets.
Cover and set the cooking time to 12 minutes.
Afterwards, use the quick release button to let the steam out.
Then serve.

Nutrition Facts
Servings: 6
Per Serving % Daily Value*
Calories 75
Total Fat 3.7g   5%
Saturated Fat 0.3g   1%
Trans Fat 0g
Cholesterol 0mg 0%
Sodium 156mg   7%
Potassium 15mg 0%
Total Carb 6.7g   2%
Dietary Fiber 1.4g   5%
Sugars 3.8g
Protein 1.7g
Vitamin A 0% · Vitamin C 1%
Calcium 0% · Iron 2%
*Based on a 2,000 calorie diet

6. Hearty Chowder

Yield: 4 Servings
Preparation Time: 25 Minutes

Ingredients
2 cups of fat-free chicken broth
2 peeled and cubed potatoes
2 cups of a whole kernel corn
2 medium sized chopped onions
1 cup of sliced celery
2 teaspoons of dried thyme leaves
1 cup of almond milk, divided into 2
4 tablespoons of cornstarch
Salt and pepper
And 8 tablespoons of water

Directions
Mix the chicken broth, potatoes, corns, onions, celery, thyme, salt, and pepper in an instant pot and cook for about 15 minutes.
Afterwards, use the natural release button to let out the steam and then add the milk. Thereafter cook it for an additional 10 minutes.
Once you are done cooking, open the pot after releasing the steam and add the cornstarch mixed with the 8 tablespoons of water.
Now stir the corn flour in the water and add it into the chowder.
Cook for an additional 5 minutes by pressing the sauté button.
Serve once it is thickened.

Nutrition Facts
Servings: 4
Per Serving% Daily Value*
Calories 355
Total Fat 16.1g   21%
Saturated Fat 13.1g   65%
Trans Fat 0g
Cholesterol 0mg 0%
Sodium 433mg   19%
Potassium 1053mg   22%

Total Carb 48.5g 16%
Dietary Fiber 7.8g   28%
Sugars 8.8g
Protein 8.9g
Vitamin A 5% · Vitamin C 53%
Calcium 4% · Iron 26%
*Based on a 2,000 calorie diet

7. Garden Stew

Yield: 6 Servings
Preparation Time: 20 Minutes

Ingredients
7 cups of vegetable broth
10 Oz of sliced mushrooms
10 Oz of florets cauliflowers
2 peeled and cubed potatoes
4 onions cut into wedges
4 tomatoes also cut in wedges
2 cloves of minced garlic
4 teaspoons of dried savory leaves
4 bay leaves
8 small sliced zucchinis
Salt and pepper
And 4 cups of warm cooked couscous

Directions
Mix all the ingredients (except for the couscous), in an instant pot.
Cover and cook for about 20 minutes.
Then release the steam using the natural release button and open the pot.
Serve the cooked stew on top of the couscous in a bowl.

Nutrition Facts
Servings: 6
Per Serving% Daily Value*
Calories 629
Total Fat 3.2g   4%

Saturated Fat 0.7g   4%
Trans Fat 0g
Cholesterol 0mg   0%
Sodium 947mg   41%
Potassium 1737mg   37%
Total Carb 123.5g   41%
Dietary Fiber 13.5g   48%
Sugars 13.5g
Protein 27.5g
Vitamin A 35% · Vitamin C 135%
Calcium 9% · Iron 27%
*Based on a 2,000 calorie diet

8. Easy Cheesy Vegetables

Yield: 5 Servings
Preparation Time: 17 Minutes

Ingredients
6 cups of washed frozen broccoli
2 cups of washed and thawed cauliflower
2 cups of sliced carrot
1 cup of chopped onion
2 cans of mushroom cream soup
3 ounces of drained chopped pimientos
2 cups of cottage cheese
Pepper
Salt
And a cooking spray, for greasing

Directions
First of all, grease the instant pot with the oil spray.
Mix all the ingredients in the pot and cook it for about 17 minutes.
Then release the steam using the natural button and open the pot.
Thereafter serve the cooked stew.

Nutrition Facts

Servings: 5
Per Serving % Daily Value*
Calories 279
Total Fat 9.3g 12%
Saturated Fat 2.7g 14%
Trans Fat 0g
Cholesterol 7mg 3%
Sodium 1233mg 54%
Potassium 934mg 20%
Total Carb 32.3g 11%
Dietary Fiber 6.4g 23%
Sugars 11.6g
Protein 19.5g
Vitamin A 350% · Vitamin C 431%
Calcium 13% · Iron 16%
*Based on a 2,000 calorie diet

9. A Simple Cooking Recipe

Yield: 6 Servings
Preparation Time 20 Minutes

Ingredients
20 Oz of frozen mixed vegetables
1 cup of a condensed cream of mushroom soup
Salt
Pepper
1 tablespoon of garlic powder
And a parsley, for garnishing

Directions
Take an instant pot and mix the vegetables, cream, salt, pepper, and garlic powder.
Cook it for about 20 minutes.
Once the vegetables are done, garnish it with parsley, and serve.

Nutrition Facts

Servings: 6
Per Serving% Daily Value*
Calories 105
Total Fat 2.7g   3%
Saturated Fat 0.6g   3%
Trans Fat 0g
Cholesterol 0mg 0%
Sodium 336mg   15%
Potassium 257mg   5%
Total Carb 16.8g 6%
Dietary Fiber 4.6g   17%
Sugars 4g
Protein 3.9g
Vitamin A 163% · Vitamin C 28%
Calcium 3% · Iron 11%
*Based on a 2,000 calorie diet

10. The Celery and Cauliflower Recipe

Yield: 6 Servings
Preparation Time: 17 Minutes

Ingredients
10 medium sized potatoes, peeled and cut into cubes
2 cups of chopped onion
6 sliced carrots
4 ribs of sliced celery
2 chicken bouillon cubes
2 tablespoons of parsley flakes
6 cups of water
1 cup of butter
And 13 Oz of Almond milk

Directions
Mix all the ingredients except for the milk in an instant pot.
Cook using a high heat pressure for about 15 minutes.
Then release the steam using the natural button and open the pot.

Thereafter press the Keep Warm button.
Open the lid and add the milk.
Stir and then serve.

Nutrition Facts
Servings: 6
Per Serving % Daily Value*
Calories 701
Total Fat 45.8g   59%
Saturated Fat 32.6g   163%
Trans Fat 0g
Cholesterol 81mg 30%
Sodium 504mg   22%
Potassium 1882mg   40%
Total Carb 69.1g 23%
Dietary Fiber 12.2g   44%
Sugars 11g
Protein 8.8g
Vitamin A 376% · Vitamin C 133%
Calcium 7% · Iron 18%
*Based on a 2,000 calorie diet

10 Graceful Meats

1. Chicken Adobo

Preparation Time: 20 Minutes
Yield: 4 Servings

Ingredients
2 pounds of chicken meat
2 tablespoons of olive oil
¼ cup of soy sauce
1/3 cup of light soy sauce
1/3 cup of vinegar
2 tablespoons of fish sauce
3 tablespoons of stevia
½ teaspoon of ground black peppercorn
2 chilies
And 2 dried bay leaves

Directions
Mix the soy sauce, light soy sauce, vinegar, stevia and the fish sauce in a medium sized bowl.
Then, add the oil to the pot and turn on the sauté button.
Heat the chicken on fire for 3 minutes till it gets brownish in color.
After that, remove the chicken from the pot.
Empty the peppercorn, red chili, and bay leave into the instant pot.
Still use the sauté button for an additional minute.
Add the sauce mixture from the bowl and then de-glaze the instant pot.
Then cook it for 15 minutes, before using the natural release button to release the steam.
Serve.

Nutrition Facts
Servings: 4
Per Serving% Daily Value*
Calories 764
Total Fat 24.4g   31%

Saturated Fat 5.8g   29%
Trans Fat 0g
Cholesterol 208mg   76%
Sodium 10672mg   464%
Potassium 714mg   15%
Total Carb 34.4g 11%
Dietary Fiber 0.3g   1%
Sugars 32.8g
Protein 85.5g
Vitamin A 7% · Vitamin C 1%
Calcium 3% · Iron 23%
*Based on a 2,000 calorie diet

2. BBQ Ribs

Preparation Time: 40 Minutes
Yield: 4 Servings

Ingredients
1 pound of baby back ribs
4 tablespoons of BBQ sauce
Grounded black pepper
Salt
And a black pepper

Directions
Remove the membrane from the ribs.
Season the ribs with the salt and ground black pepper.
Pour 1 cup of a cold running tap water and a trivet into the instant pot.
Then place the ribs on top of the trivet.
Close the instant pot lid and cook it at a high pressure for 25 minutes.
Then use the natural release button to release the steam.
Open the lid of the instant pot.
Adjust your oven to 450 degrees F and put the BBQ sauce there for about 15 minutes.
Thereafter you can then serve.

Nutrition Facts
Servings: 4
Per Serving % Daily Value*
Calories 276
Total Fat 13.9g   18%
Saturated Fat 5.6g   28%
Trans Fat 0g
Cholesterol 87mg   32%
Sodium 294mg   13%
Potassium 465mg   10%
Total Carb 5.7g   2%
Dietary Fiber 0.1g   0%
Sugars 4.1g
Protein 29.9g
Vitamin A 1% · Vitamin C 0%
Calcium 1% · Iron 16%
*Based on a 2,000 calorie diet

3. Instant Pot Roasted Beef

Preparation Time: 25 Minutes
Yield: 5 Servings

Ingredients
6 pounds of beef
1 cup of brown gravy mix
6 tablespoons of salad dressing mix
1 cup of dry ranch dressing mix
And 1 cup of water

Directions
Mix the brown gravy mix with the ranch mix, dressing mix and water in a bowl and rub it on the the meat.
Place the beef into the instant pot.
Set timer to 25 minutes.
Then release it using the natural method.
Serve and enjoy.

Nutrition Facts
Servings: 4
Per Serving % Daily Value*
Calories 1430
Total Fat 47.1g   60%
Saturated Fat 17.6g   88%
Trans Fat 0g
Cholesterol 609mg   221%
Sodium 2460mg 107%
Potassium 2804mg   60%
Total Carb 28g   9%
Dietary Fiber 2.1g   8%
Sugars 9.1g
Protein 211.3g
Vitamin A 24% · Vitamin C 4%
Calcium 9% · Iron 714%
*Based on a 2,000 calorie diet

4. Ginger and Soy Chicken

Yield: 5 Servings
Cooking Time: 15 Minutes

Ingredients
4 pounds of disjointed chicken wings, with tips
1/3 cup of soy sauce
2 tablespoons of stevia
2 tablespoons of minced ginger root
2 cloves of minced garlic
And ½ Oz. of five-spice powder

Directions
Mix the soy sauce, stevia, ginger, garlic and the five spice powders in a bowl
Massage it all over the chicken.
Pour 1 cup of cold water and a trivet into the instant pot.
Then place the chicken on top of the trivet.

Close the instant pot lid and press the meat stew button to turn on the instant pot.
Cook at a high pressure for 15 minutes.
Then use the natural release to let the steam out.
Open the lid of the instant pot.
Adjust your oven to 450degrees F.
Leave it in the oven for about 10 minutes.
Remove and serve.

Nutrition Facts
Servings: 5
Per Serving% Daily Value*
Calories 707
Total Fat 26.9g   35%
Saturated Fat 7.4g   37%
Trans Fat 0g
Cholesterol 323mg   117%
Sodium 1271mg   55%
Potassium 930mg   20%
Total Carb 2.3g   1%
Dietary Fiber 0.8g   3%
Sugars 0.3g
Protein 106.5g
Vitamin A 6% · Vitamin C 1%
Calcium 5% · Iron 27%
*Based on a 2,000 calorie diet

5. Simple Beef Stew

Preparation Time: 25 Minuets
Yield: 6 Servings

Ingredients
4 pounds of cubed lean beef stew
4 cups of plum tomatoes,
½ cup of beef broth
1 cup of minced medium onions

2 cloves of garlic
Then salt and pepper

Directions
Mix all the ingredients in an instant pot.
Press the meat stew button to turn on the instant pot and cook at a high pressure for 25 minutes.
Let the steam out using the natural method.
Serve and enjoy the simplest dish of beef.

Nutrition Facts
Servings: 6
Per Serving% Daily Value*
Calories 598
Total Fat 18.4g   24%
Saturated Fat 0.1g   0%
Trans Fat 0g
Cholesterol 0mg 0%
Sodium 80mg   3%
Potassium 305mg   6%
Total Carb 9g   3%
Dietary Fiber 1.9g   7%
Sugars 6g
Protein 98.2g
Vitamin A 26% · Vitamin C 50%
Calcium 2% · Iron 4%
*Based on a 2,000 calorie diet

6. Coconut Beef Curry

Preparation Time: 35 Minutes
Yield: 6 Servings

Ingredients
1 tablespoon of red chili powder
2 greens of finely chopped chilies
3 pounds of cubed beef

3 cups of coconut milk
4 cups of beef broth
2 teaspoons of cumin
1 tablespoon of coriander
2 tablespoons of olive oil
1 chopped onion
And 1 cup of chopped cherry tomatoes

Directions
Turn the sauté button of instant pot on and add the oil.
Once it gets hot, add the onions and let it there for a while.
Thereafter, add the beef, green chilies, red chilies, cumin, and coriander.
Next, pour in the broth, tomatoes and let it cook for 5 minutes.
Then, press the meat stew button to turn on the instant pot.
Then close the lid and set the timer to 20 minutes.
After 20 minutes use the natural release button to let the steam out
Open the pot and then add the coconut milk.
Stir twice and cook for an additional 5 minutes by turning the sauté button on.
Once the gray is thickened, serve and enjoy.

Nutrition Facts
Servings: 6
Per Serving % Daily Value*
Calories 783
Total Fat 48.8g   63%
Saturated Fat 31.7g   158%
Trans Fat 0g
Cholesterol 203mg   74%
Sodium 692mg   30%
Potassium 1505mg   32%
Total Carb 11.3g   4%
Dietary Fiber 3.9g   14%
Sugars 6.2g
Protein 75.5g
Vitamin A 23% · Vitamin C 16%
Calcium 4% · Iron 254%
*Based on a 2,000 calorie diet

7. Beetroot and Beef Stew

Preparation Time: 30 Minuets
Yield: 6 Servings

Ingredients
2 cups of peeled and cubed Beetroots
2 cups of beef broth
1 tablespoon of red chilies
1/3 teaspoon of black pepper
Salt and pepper
And 3 pounds of cube sized beef

Directions
Empty all the listed ingredients into an instant pot.
Press the meat stew button on the instant pot and cook for about 30 minutes.
Quickly release the steam.
Open the pot and serve.

Nutrition Facts
Servings: 6
Per Serving% Daily Value*
Calories 462
Total Fat 14.7g   19%
Saturated Fat 5.5g   27%
Trans Fat 0g
Cholesterol 203mg   74%
Sodium 448mg   19%
Potassium 1164mg   25%
Total Carb 6.6g   2%
Dietary Fiber 1.4g   5%
Sugars 4.9g
Protein 71.5g
Vitamin A 4% · Vitamin C 4%
Calcium 1% · Iron 241%
*Based on a 2,000 calorie diet

8. Steak and Gravy

Preparation Time: 25 Minutes
Yield: 6 Servings

Ingredients
2 pounds of cubed steak
Salt and pepper
1 pack of onion gravy mix
1 cup of Almond flour, for dredging
1 can cream of mushroom soup
3 of cups water
And 1 tablespoon of olive oil

Directions
Sprinkle the salt and pepper on the steak and then deepen it in the almond flour.
Turn on the sauté button of the instant pot and then add the oil.
Let it cook for a few seconds and then add the steak.
Let the steak cook until it gets brown.
Press the meat stew button to turn on the instant pot.
Pour in all the remaining listed ingredients.
Close the pot and set the timer to 25 minutes.
Then quickly release the steam.
Afterwards, open the pot and serve.

Nutrition Facts
Servings: 6
Per Serving % Daily Value*
Calories 407
Total Fat 15.4g   20%
Saturated Fat 3.8g   19%
Trans Fat 0g
Cholesterol 136mg   49%
Sodium 671mg   29%
Potassium 536mg   11%
Total Carb 6.8g   2%
Dietary Fiber 0.5g   2%

Sugars 0.7g
Protein 57.2g
Vitamin A 0% · Vitamin C 0%
Calcium 1% · Iron 31%
*Based on a 2,000 calorie diet

9. Beef with Apricots

Preparation Time: 25 Minutes
Yield: 6 Servings

Ingredients
2 large red onions, sliced into thin wedges
4 chopped parsnips
1.5 kg of boneless beef brisket
Salt and black pepper
2 teaspoons of grounded coriander
2 tablespoons of grounded cumin
1 teaspoon of grounded cinnamon
1 teaspoon of garlic powder
Pinch of nutmeg
2 cups of dried apricots
300 ml of dry red wine
And 4 cups of low sodium beef stock

Directions
Place the onion and parsnip in the bottom of an instant pot.
Season the beef with salt and pepper using a bowl.
Also with a small bowl, mix the nutmeg, garlic, cinnamon, coriander, and cumin.
Rub the spice mixture over the beef.
Now place the beef on top of the parsnip in the pot.
Then place the apricots, wine, and stock.
Press the meat stew button to turn on the instant pot.
Cook it for about 25 minutes at a high pressure.
Once done, serve and enjoy.

Nutrition Facts
Servings: 4
Per Serving% Daily Value*
Calories 906
Total Fat 24.9g   32%
Saturated Fat 8.9g   45%
Trans Fat 0g
Cholesterol 335mg   122%
Sodium 477mg   21%
Potassium 2209mg   47%
Total Carb 31.9g 11%
Dietary Fiber 7.1g   25%
Sugars 14.2g
Protein 120.1g
Vitamin A 52% · Vitamin C 41%
Calcium 7% · Iron 410%
*Based on a 2,000 calorie diet

10. Gravy Chicken

Preparation Time: 25 Minutes
Yield: 4 Servings

Ingredients
4 pounds of boneless chicken with its leg pieces
4 tablespoons of dark brown sugar
2 teaspoons of grounded ginger
½ cup of soy sauce
2 tablespoons of ketchup
2 cloves of crushed garlic
And a Salt with a freshly grounded black pepper

Preparation
Take an instant pot and pour all the ingredients into it.
Press the meat stew button to turn on the instant pot.
Cook it for about 25 minutes at a high pressure.
Once done, serve and enjoy.

Nutrition Facts
Servings: 4
Per Serving % Daily Value*
Calories 749
Total Fat 13.8g 18%
Saturated Fat 3.9g 19%
Trans Fat 0g
Cholesterol 349mg 127%
Sodium 2169mg 94%
Potassium 976mg 21%
Total Carb 14.3g 5%
Dietary Fiber 0.4g 2%
Sugars 11g
Protein 133.8g
Vitamin A 5% · Vitamin C 3%
Calcium 6% · Iron 27%
*Based on a 2,000 calorie diet

10 Great Lunches

1. Fish and Tomato Stew

Preparation Time: 15 Minutes
Yield: 4 Servings

Ingredient
½ cup of water
1 cup of tomato sauce
2 cups of chopped tomatoes
4 chopped onions
½ cup of green bell pepper
2 teaspoons of garlic
1 teaspoon of oregano leaves
4 pounds of sliced whitefish steaks
Then salt and pepper

Directions
Mix all the listed ingredients in an instant pot.
Adjust the timer manually to 15 minutes.
Open the pot using the natural release to let the steam out.
Serve the stew and enjoy.

Nutrition Facts
Servings: 4
Per Serving% Daily Value*
Calories 75817
Total Fat 4245.3g   5443%
Saturated Fat 1106.6g   5533%
Trans Fat 0g
Cholesterol 29024mg   10554%
Sodium 35704mg   1552%
Potassium 617mg   13%
Total Carb 18.9g 6%
Dietary Fiber 4.8g   17%
Sugars 10.4g

Protein 8723.9g
Vitamin A 50% · Vitamin C 90%
Calcium 4% · Iron 8%
*Based on a 2,000 calorie diet

2. Instant Pot Fettuccine with Seafood

Yield: 4 Servings
Preparation Time: 15 Minutes

Ingredients
1/3 cup of dry white wine
2 cups of chopped tomatoes
1/3 cup of green bell pepper and onion,
½ cup of sliced mushrooms
2 cloves of minced garlic
1 tablespoon of tomato paste
2 teaspoons of oregano
1 teaspoon of basil leaves
1 teaspoon of ground turmeric
6 ounces of sea scallops
3 Oz of sliced crab meat
3 Oz of cubed haddock steak
Salt, pepper
And 10 ounces of cooked fettuccine

Directions
Place all the listed ingredients in an instant pot (excluding the fettuccine) and set the timer to 15 minutes.
Once cooked, use the natural button to release the steam.
Serve over the fettuccine.

Nutrition Facts
Servings: 4
Per Serving   % Daily Value*
Calories 1795
Total Fat 13.4g   17%

Saturated Fat 2.5g   13%
Trans Fat 0g
Cholesterol 1140mg   414%
Sodium 1505mg 65%
Potassium 6227mg   132%
Total Carb 47.4g 16%
Dietary Fiber 1.9g   7%
Sugars 3.7g
Protein 359.3g
Vitamin A 42% · Vitamin C 58%
Calcium 55% · Iron 141%
*Based on a 2,000 calorie diet

3. Shrimp and Vegetable Stew

Yield: 4 Servings
Preparation Time: 12 Minutes

Ingredients
2 cups of stew tomatoes
4 ounces of thickly sliced turkey sausage
1 cup of baby carrot
1 cup of Brussels sprouts
1 cup of kernel corn
4 onions cut into thin wedges
2 teaspoons of chili powder
5 ounces of peeled shrimp
Then salt and pepper

Directions
Mix all the listed ingredients in instant pot and cook using a low heat pressure for 12 minutes.
Quickly release the steam.
Serve.

Nutrition Facts
Servings: 4
Per Serving% Daily Value*

Calories 253
Total Fat 9.5g 12%
Saturated Fat 2.9g 15%
Trans Fat 0.1g
Cholesterol 98mg 36%
Sodium 496mg 22%
Potassium 668mg 14%
Total Carb 26.1g 9%
Dietary Fiber 5.8g 21%
Sugars 9.6g
Protein 17.5g
Vitamin A 45% · Vitamin C 59%
Calcium 7% · Iron 14%
*Based on a 2,000 calorie diet

4. Slow-Cooker Pork Chops

Preparation Time: 20 Minutes
Yield: 6 Servings

Ingredients
6 pork loin chops
1/3 teaspoon of grounded black pepper
4 cloves of finely chopped garlic
1 cup of creamy mushroom soup
4 tablespoons of cornstarch
And 4 tablespoons of water

Directions
Mix all the listed ingredients in an instant pot and set it manually to 20 minutes.
Quickly release the steam.
Serve and enjoy.

Nutrition Facts
Servings: 6
Per Serving % Daily Value*

Calories 297
Total Fat 20.6g   26%
Saturated Fat 8g 40%
Trans Fat 0g
Cholesterol 70mg   26%
Sodium 189mg   8%
Potassium 285mg   6%
Total Carb 7.9g   3%
Dietary Fiber 0.5g   2%
Sugars 0.4g
Protein 18.6g
Vitamin A 1% · Vitamin C 2%
Calcium 2% · Iron 5%
*Based on a 2,000 calorie diet

5. Pork and Squash Ragout

Preparation Time: 20 Minutes
Yield: 6 Servings

Ingredients
2 pounds of boneless beef
4 cups of diced tomatoes
2 cups of drained red kidney beans
2 cups of peeled and cubed butternut
2 cups of onions
1/3 cup of green bell peppers
2 teaspoons of minced garlic
Then salt and pepper

Directions
Mix all the listed ingredients in an instant pot and set the timer to 20 minutes.
Then, quick release the steam.
Serve and enjoy.

Nutrition Facts

Servings: 6
Per Serving % Daily Value*
Calories 1136
Total Fat 29.4g   38%
Saturated Fat 10.8g   54%
Trans Fat 0g
Cholesterol 406mg   147%
Sodium 318mg   14%
Potassium 3340mg   71%
Total Carb 58.6g 20%
Dietary Fiber 15.4g   55%
Sugars 8.6g
Protein 154.1g
Vitamin A 49% · Vitamin C 106%
Calcium 6% · Iron 521%
*Based on a 2,000 calorie diet

6. Ginger Pumpkin Chicken Soup

Preparation Time: 20 Minutes
Yield: 4 Servings

Ingredients
4 cups of Chicken broth
1 cup of peeled and seeded pumpkin
½ cup of onion
1 tablespoon of chopped Ginger root
1 teaspoon of minced garlic
⅓ cup of chicken stock
½ teaspoon of grounded cloves
Then salt and pepper

Directions
Mix all the listed ingredients in the instant pot and cook using a high pressure for about 20 minutes.
Quickly release the steam.
Once done serve and enjoy.

Nutrition Facts
Servings: 4
Per Serving % Daily Value*
Calories 71
Total Fat 1.7g 2%
Saturated Fat 0.5g 3%
Trans Fat 0g
Cholesterol 0mg 0%
Sodium 832mg 36%
Potassium 376mg 8%
Total Carb 8.4g 3%
Dietary Fiber 2.4g 8%
Sugars 3.5g
Protein 5.9g
Vitamin A 318% · Vitamin C 6%
Calcium 3% · Iron 9%
*Based on a 2,000 calorie diet

7. Zucchini Casserole Recipe

Preparation Time: 15 Minutes
Yield: 6 Servings

Ingredients
2 eggs
½ cup of milk
3 cup of almond flour
2 pounds of finely chopped zucchini
2 Oz. of sliced mushrooms
3 tablespoons of chives
2 cloves of minced garlic
1/3 teaspoon of dried Italian seasoning
¼ teaspoon of salt
1/4 teaspoon of pepper
And a 1/2 cup of shredded Parmesan cheese

Directions

Take a bowl; beat the eggs, milk, almond flour, salt and pepper into it.
Then add all the remaining listed ingredients excluding the cheese.
Pour the mixture into a casserole (dish of glass).
Sprinkle it with the Parmesan.
Place it on a rack using an instant cooker.
Cover and cook it on a high pressure for about 13 minutes.
Serve.

Nutrition Facts

Servings: 6
Per Serving % Daily Value*
Calories 114
Total Fat 6.7g   9%
Saturated Fat 1.8g   9%
Trans Fat 0g
Cholesterol 60mg   22%
Sodium 214mg   9%
Potassium 489mg   10%
Total Carb 8.3g   3%
Dietary Fiber 2.5g   9%
Sugars 4.2g
Protein 7.6g
Vitamin A 16% · Vitamin C 45%
Calcium 9% · Iron 8%
*Based on a 2,000 caloric diet

8. Curry-Spiced Nuts

Preparation Time: 15 Minutes
Yield: 4 Servings

Ingredients

6 cups of mixed nuts
4 tablespoons of melted butter
2 tablespoons of stevia

2 teaspoons of curry powder
1 teaspoon of garlic powder
And 1 teaspoon of grounded cinnamon

Directions
Pour all the listed ingredients into the instant pot and adjust the timer to 8-10 minutes.
Turn the heat to a low pressure to keep it warm for 2 minutes.
Remove the dish from the pot and let it cool.
Serve.

Nutrition Facts
Servings: 4
Per Serving % Daily Value*
Calories 1437
Total Fat 133g   171%
Saturated Fat 26.9g   135%
Trans Fat 0g
Cholesterol 31mg 11%
Sodium 744mg   32%
Potassium 1204mg   26%
Total Carb 49.7g 17%
Dietary Fiber 12.6g   45%
Sugars 9.7g
Protein 33.9g
Vitamin A 13% · Vitamin C 2%
Calcium 19% · Iron 33%
*Based on a 2,000 calorie diet

9. Eggplant Caviar

Preparation Time: 5 Minutes
Yield: 4 Servings

Ingredients
1 large eggplant
1/3 cup of a finely chopped tomato

½ cup of chopped onion,
1 cup of reduced-fat yogurt
3 cloves of minced garlic
2 tablespoons of olive oil
1 tablespoon of oregano leaves
2 tablespoons of lemon juice
Then salt and pepper

Directions
Place the eggplant in an instant pot and cook it for about 5 minutes until it gets soft.
Open the lid and quickly release the steam.
Take out the eggs and then mash it with all the remaining ingredients.
Serve and enjoy.

Nutrition Facts
Servings: 4
Per Serving % Daily Value*
Calories 180
Total Fat 8.2g   11%
Saturated Fat 1.7g   9%
Trans Fat 0g
Cholesterol 4mg 1%
Sodium 52mg   2%
Potassium 575mg   12%
Total Carb 21.3g 7%
Dietary Fiber 5.2g   19%
Sugars 9.2g
Protein 6.5g
Vitamin A 6% · Vitamin C 29%
Calcium 14% · Iron 5%
*Based on a 2,000 calorie diet

10. Instant Pot Chicken

Preparation Time: 35-40 Minutes
Yield: 4 Servings

Ingredients

2 pounds of a whole organic chicken
1 tablespoon of coconut oil
1 teaspoon of paprika
1 cup of organic bone broth (Chicken)
1 teaspoon of dried thyme
Black pepper
2 tablespoons of lemon juice
Salt
And 4 cloves of peeled garlic

Directions

Rub all the seasoning over the chicken.
Press the sauté button on the instant pot and heat the oil.
Then add the chicken and cook it for 7 minutes.
Afterwards quickly release the steam and open the pot.
Flip the chicken; add the broth and lemon juice along with the garlic.
Lock the lid and adjust it to 25 minutes on a high pressure.
Let the pressure cooker release naturally.
Serve.

Nutrition Facts

Servings: 4
Per Serving % Daily Value*
Calories 389
Total Fat 10.4g   13%
Saturated Fat 5g 25%
Trans Fat 0g
Cholesterol 175mg   64%
Sodium 208mg   9%
Potassium 460mg   10%
Total Carb 1.6g   1%
Dietary Fiber 0.4g   1%
Sugars 0.2g
Protein 68.3g
Vitamin A 11% · Vitamin C 8%
Calcium 3% · Iron 14%
*Based on a 2,000 calorie diet

10 Yummy Desserts

1. Gingerbread Cake

Preparation Time: 15 Minutes
Yield: 4 Servings

Ingredients
2 cups of almond flour
1/3 cup of all-purpose flour
2 teaspoons of grounded cinnamon
1 teaspoon of grounded ginger
A pinch of salt
10 tablespoons of butter
6 scoops of stevia
1 whisked egg
½ cup of almond milk
And a ½ teaspoon of baking soda

Directions
Place a steamer basket in the instant pot and add about 2 cups of water.
Use an Oil spray, and spray a cake pan.
Take a bowl and pour the flours, salt, spices into it.
Mix the butter, stevia in a glass and microwave it for 30 seconds.
Once margarine is melted, pour it into the flour mixture.
Then add the whisked egg.
Next, add the milk and baking soda until it blends properly.
Pour the batter into the greased cake pan.
Place the pan in a steamer basket.
Cover the locking lid of the instant pot and select the high pressure for 15 minutes.
When the instant pot timer beeps, turn it off.
After a minute, use a quick pressure release.
Open the lid of the pot and remove the cake from the steamer basket.
Serve once it gets cool.

Nutrition Facts

Servings: 4
Per Serving% Daily Value*
Calories 466
Total Fat 43.8g   56%
Saturated Fat 25.5g   127%
Trans Fat 0g
Cholesterol 117mg   43%
Sodium 427mg   19%
Potassium 124mg   3%
Total Carb 14g   5%
Dietary Fiber 3.1g   11%
Sugars 1.2g
Protein 6.5g
Vitamin A 31% · Vitamin C 2%
Calcium 3% · Iron 7%
*Based on a 2,000 calorie diet

2. Chocolate Chip Peanut Butter Cake

Preparation Time: 15 Minutes
Yield: 7 Servings

Ingredients
1/3 cup of butter
6 scoops of stevia
2 eggs
1/2 cup of peanut butter
2 cups of self-rising flour
1/4 teaspoon of salt
½ cup of chocolate morsels
And 2 cups of hot fudge

Directions
Place a steamer basket in the instant pot and add about 2 cups of water.
Moist a cake pan with an oil spray
Beat the butter and stevia in a bowl and add the eggs.

Beat all the ingredients properly to avoid unequal reactions.
Pour in the peanut butter, flour, salt, and chocolate morsels.
Then pour the batter into the greased cake pan.
Place the pan in a steamer basket.
Cover the locking lid of the instant pot and select a high pressure for 15 minutes.
When the instant pot timer beeps, turn it off.
After a minute, use a quick pressure release.
Open the lid of the pot and remove the cake from the steamer basket.
Once it is cool, serve it with the hot fudge sauce.

Nutrition Facts
Servings: 8
Per Serving % Daily Value*
Calories 536
Total Fat 20g	26%
Saturated Fat 8.6g	43%
Trans Fat 0g
Cholesterol 63mg	23%
Sodium 275mg	12%
Potassium 323mg	7%
Total Carb 80.5g 27%
Dietary Fiber 3.8g	13%
Sugars 42.9g
Protein 10.3g
Vitamin A 10% · Vitamin C 0%
Calcium 2% · Iron 26%
*Based on a 2,000 calorie diet

3. Five-Layer Bars

Preparation Time: 15 Minutes
Yield: 8 Servings

Ingredients
1 and 1/2 cup of graham cracker crumbs
1 tablespoon of butter

1 tablespoon of stevia
2/3 cup of semi-sweet chocolate morsels
1/3 cup of flaked coconut
1/3 cup of walnuts
And 1 can of condensed milk

Directions
Mix the graham cracker crumbs, butter and stevia in a bowl and press it into the bottom of the spring form pan.
Sprinkle it with the chocolate morsels, coconut, and walnuts.
Drop some little amount of the condense milk over the top.
Place the pan on the rack of the instant pot.
Cover the locking lid of the instant pot and select a high pressure for 15 minutes.
When the instant pot timer beeps, turn it off.
After a minute, use a quick pressure release.
Open the lid of the pot and remove the cake from the rack.
Serve once it gets cool.

Nutrition Facts
Servings: 8
Per Serving % Daily Value*
Calories 587
Total Fat 20.9g   27%
Saturated Fat 8.4g   42%
Trans Fat 0g
Cholesterol 26mg   10%
Sodium 599mg   26%
Potassium 40mg 1%
Total Carb 92.2g 31%
Dietary Fiber 5.3g   19%
Sugars 52.1g
Protein 9.6g
Vitamin A 7% · Vitamin C 3%
Calcium 12% · Iron 18%
*Based on a 2,000 calorie diet

4. Easy Brownies

Preparation Time: 15 Minutes
Yield: 6 Servings

Ingredients
20 Oz of Brownie mix
4 tablespoons of melted butter
And 1 cup of chopped walnuts

Directions
Mix all the ingredients in a bowl.
Pour the batter into the greased 7-inch pan and place it on a rack in a 6-quart instant pot.
Cover and cook it on a high pressure for 15 minutes.
After a minute, use the quick pressure release.
Open the lid of the pot and remove cake from the rack.
Serve once it is cool.

Nutrition Facts
Nutrition Facts
Servings: 6
Per Serving% Daily Value*
Calories 607
Total Fat 34.1g   44%
Saturated Fat 7.9g   40%
Trans Fat 0g
Cholesterol 20mg   7%
Sodium 341mg   15%
Potassium 318mg   7%
Total Carb 74.5g 25%
Dietary Fiber 1.4g   5%
Sugars 0.2g
Protein 8.9g
Vitamin A 9% · Vitamin C 1%
Calcium 3% · Iron 14%
*Based on a 2,000 calorie diet

5. Lemon Cream Cheese Bites

Preparation Time: 12 Minutes
Yield: 4 Servings

Ingredients
9 Oz of yellow cake mix
1 egg
1 tablespoon of butter
4 ounces of cream cheese
4 tablespoons of stevia
½ teaspoon of vanilla
1 tablespoon of lemon zest
And a 1/4 teaspoon of salt

Directions
Beat the cream cheese, stevia, and vanilla in a bowl until it gets smoothened.
Then add the flour, zest, egg, butter, and salt.
Pour it into the pan.
Place the pan on the rack in a 6-quart instant pot.
Cover and cook it on a high pressure for 12 minutes.
Then cut it into squares or wedges and serve.

Nutrition Facts
Servings: 4
Per Serving% Daily Value*
Calories 418
Total Fat 21.3g   27%
Saturated Fat 9.5g   48%
Trans Fat 0g
Cholesterol 81mg 29%
Sodium 686mg   30%
Potassium 107mg   2%
Total Carb 51g   17%
Dietary Fiber 0.8g   3%
Sugars 27.9g
Protein 6.4g

Vitamin A 18% · Vitamin C 3%
Calcium 9% · Iron 8%
*Based on a 2,000 calorie diet

6. Rhubarb-Strawberry Compote

Preparation Time: 12 Minutes
Yield: 4 Servings

Ingredients
1 pound of strawberries
1 pound of rhubarb
1/2 cup of stevia
And a 1/4 cup water

Directions
Mix all ingredients in an instant pot
Cover and cook it on a high pressure for 12 minutes.
If you need to get it more thickened then, press the sauté button and leave it there for an additional 5 minutes.
Serve and enjoy.

Nutrition Facts
Servings: 4
Per Serving % Daily Value*
Calories 60
Total Fat 0.6g   1%
Saturated Fat 0.1g   0%
Trans Fat 0g
Cholesterol 0mg 0%
Sodium 6mg   0%
Potassium 500mg   11%
Total Carb 13.9g 5%
Dietary Fiber 4.3g   15%
Sugars 6.8g
Protein 1.8g
Vitamin A 4% · Vitamin C 126%

Calcium 9% · Iron 4%
*Based on a 2,000 calorie diet

7. Baked Apples

Preparation Time: 7 Minutes
Yield: 4 Servings

Ingredient
4 large baking apples
½ cup of dried fruit
4 tablespoons of toasted pecans
5 tablespoons of stevia
1/3 teaspoon of grounded cinnamon
1/6 teaspoon of grounded nutmeg
And 4 tablespoons of butter

Directions
Centralize the apples.
Mix all the remaining listed ingredients in a bowl.
Fill apples with the mixed ingredients and place it in an instant pot.
Cover and cook it using a high pressure for 7 minutes.
Serve.

Nutrition Facts
Servings: 4
Per Serving % Daily Value*
Calories 237
Total Fat 12.1g   16%
Saturated Fat 7.3g   37%
Trans Fat 0g
Cholesterol 31mg 11%
Sodium 84mg   4%
Potassium 244mg   5%
Total Carb 35.3g 12%
Dietary Fiber 5.8g   21%
Sugars 27.1g
Protein 0.8g

Vitamin A 12% · Vitamin C 28%
Calcium 1% · Iron 6%
*Based on a 2,000 calorie diet

8 Chocolate Fondue

Preparation Time: 7 Minutes
Yield: 8 Servings

Ingredients
32 Oz of dark chocolate
1 cup of light cream
4 tablespoons of rum
And a dipper: whole strawberries, fruit pieces

Directions
Mix all chocolate and light cream in an instant pot.
Cover and cook it for 7 minutes.
Thereafter open it and add the rum.
 Serve with dippers (not included in nutritional analysis).

Nutrition Facts
Servings: 8
Per Serving % Daily Value*
Calories 667
Total Fat 38.3g   49%
Saturated Fat 26.5g   132%
Trans Fat 0g
Cholesterol 43mg   16%
Sodium 95mg   4%
Potassium 437mg   9%
Total Carb 67.8g 23%
Dietary Fiber 3.9g   14%
Sugars 58.4g
Protein 9g
Vitamin A 12% · Vitamin C 0%
Calcium 17% · Iron 15%
*Based on a 2,000 calorie diet

9. Winter Fruit Compote

Preparation Time: 7 Minutes
Yield: 10 Servings

Ingredients
10 Oz of Dried fruit
6 Oz of Pears
1/3 of thinly sliced lemon
1 cup of apple juice
½ tablespoon of cinnamon
½ tablespoon of whole cloves
And 1/8 teaspoon of salt

Directions
Mix all ingredients in an instant pot.
 Cover and cook it on high pressure for 7 minutes.
Serve it warm.

Nutrition Facts
Servings: 1
Per Serving% Daily Value*
Calories 507
Total Fat 2.3g   3%
Saturated Fat 0.6g   3%
Trans Fat 0g
Cholesterol 0mg 0%
Sodium 324mg   14%
Potassium 572mg   12%
Total Carb 129.8g   43%
Dietary Fiber 13.8g   49%
Sugars 103.3g
Protein 1.6g
Vitamin A 3% · Vitamin C 44%
Calcium 8% · Iron 8%
*Based on a 2,000 calorie diet

10. Rum Raisin Caramel Fondue

Preparation Time: 5 Minutes
Yield: 8 Servings

Ingredients
2 cups of caramel ice cream topping
1/3 cup of marshmallow cream
½ cup of raisins
And 2 tablespoons of light rum

Directions
Mix all the ingredients in an instant pot.
Cover and cook it on a high pressure for 5 minutes.
Serve it warm.

Nutrition Facts
Servings: 8
Per Serving% Daily Value*
Calories 268
Total Fat 0.1g   0%
Saturated Fat 0.1g   1%
Trans Fat 0g
Cholesterol 1mg   0%
Sodium 294mg   13%
Potassium 137mg   3%
Total Carb 67.7g 23%
Dietary Fiber 1.1g   4%
Sugars 9.2g
Protein 1.6g
Vitamin A 2% · Vitamin C 1%
Calcium 4% · Iron 2%
*Based on a 2,000 calorie diet

10 Flavored Dinners

1. Karelian Ragout

Preparation Time: 25 Minutes
Yield: 4 Servings

Ingredients
1 pound of pork loin
2 cups of beef broth
2 cups of onions
1/3 teaspoon of grounded allspice
Salt and pepper
And a 1/4 cup of finely chopped parsley for garnishing

Directions
Mix all the ingredients in a 6-quart Instant pot.
Cover and cook it for 25 minutes.
Remove the bay leaves.
And serve it, after being garnished with the parsley.

Nutrition Facts
Servings: 4
Per Serving% Daily Value*
Calories 318
Total Fat 16.6g   21%
Saturated Fat 6.1g   31%
Trans Fat 0g
Cholesterol 91mg 33%
Sodium 456mg   20%
Potassium 690mg   15%
Total Carb 6.2g   2%
Dietary Fiber 1.4g   5%
Sugars 2.8g
Protein 34.2g
Vitamin A 11% · Vitamin C 16%
Calcium 4% · Iron 9%
*Based on a 2,000 calorie diet

2. Three-Meat Goulash

Preparation Time: 25 Minutes
Yield: 4 Servings

Ingredients
12 Oz of a boneless beef eye
1 cup of chicken breast
1 cup of pork lion
1 cup of beef broth
1/3 cup of tomato paste
2 large coarsely chopped tomatoes
10 Oz of sliced mushrooms
½ cup of chopped green onions
1 tablespoon of paprika
3/4 teaspoon of caraway seeds
¾ cup of reduced-fat sour cream
3 tablespoons of cornstarch
Salt, pepper
And noodles, side servings (not included in nutritional information)

Directions
Mix all the ingredients, except for the sour cream and cornstarch in an instant pot.
Cover and cook it for 25 minutes.
Open the pot and then add the sour cream and cornstarch.
Stir until it gets thickened.
Serve on top of the noodles.

Nutrition Facts
Servings: 4
Per Serving% Daily Value*
Calories 1212
Total Fat 79.5g   102%
Saturated Fat 31.1g   155%
Trans Fat 3g
Cholesterol 287mg   104%
Sodium 699mg   30%

Potassium 1271mg 27%
Total Carb 27.9g 9%
Dietary Fiber 4.1g 15%
Sugars 8g
Protein 97.1g
Vitamin A 83% · Vitamin C 43%
Calcium 8% · Iron 51%
*Based on a 2,000 calorie diet

3. Family Beef Stew

Preparation Time: 30 Minutes
Yield: 4 Servings

Ingredients
2 pounds of beef round steak, cut into strips
2 cups of beef broth
2 small onions cut into wedges
2 thickly sliced carrots
1 teaspoon of dried thyme leaves
Then salt and pepper

Preparation
Mix all the listed ingredients in an instant pot and cover it.
Prepare it for 30 minutes.
Then serve.

Nutrition Facts
Servings: 4
Per Serving% Daily Value*
Calories 538
Total Fat 20.9g 27%
Saturated Fat 7.2g 36%
Trans Fat 0g
Cholesterol 191mg 69%
Sodium 548mg 24%
Potassium 1297mg 28%

Total Carb 7.9g   3%
Dietary Fiber 2g   7%
Sugars 3.4g
Protein 75.2g
Vitamin A 223% · Vitamin C 21%
Calcium 5% · Iron 41%
*Based on a 2,000 calorie diet

4. Plain Meat Loaf

Preparation Time: 30 Minutes
Yield: 4 Servings

Ingredients
2 pounds of lean ground beef
½ cup of almond milk
1 egg
¼ cup of chili sauce
½ cup of chopped onion
½ cup of green bell pepper
1 teaspoon of garlic
1 teaspoon of Italian seasoning
1 teaspoon of salt
And a ½ teaspoon of pepper

Directions
Make the foil handles and place it into the instant pot.
Mix all the ingredients until it blends properly; then carve the mixture into a loaf shape.
Place the loaf into the instant pot.
Make sure the sides of loaf do not touch the instant pot.
Cover and cook it for 30 minutes.
Remove, using the foil handles.
Then serve.

Nutrition Facts
Servings: 4

Per Serving % Daily Value*
Calories 523
Total Fat 22.8g   29%
Saturated Fat 12.1g   60%
Trans Fat 0g
Cholesterol 244mg   89%
Sodium 1133mg   49%
Potassium 1084mg   23%
Total Carb 5g   2%
Dietary Fiber 1.3g   5%
Sugars 2.7g
Protein 71.3g
Vitamin A 19% · Vitamin C 69%
Calcium 2% · Iron 242%
*Based on a 2,000 calorie diet

5. Lemon Meat Loaf

Preparation Time: 30 Minutes
Yield: 4 Servings

Main Ingredients
2 pounds of lean ground beef
1 cup of fresh bread crumbs
2 eggs
1/3 cup of onion
1 clove of minced garlic
1 tablespoon of lemon juice
1 tablespoon of grated lemon zest
2 teaspoons of Dijon mustard
1/2 teaspoon of black pepper
And 3/4 teaspoon of salt

Egg Lemon Sauce recipe
1 tablespoon of butter
2 tablespoons of almond flour
1/2 cup of chicken broth

1 lightly beaten egg
5 tablespoons of lemon juice
½ teaspoon of grated lemon zest
Then salt and white pepper

Directions
Make the foil handles and place it in the instant pot.
Mix all the ingredients until it blends properly; carve the mixture into a loaf shape.
Place the loaf in the pot.
Make sure the sides of the loaf do not touch the instant pot.
Cover and cook it for 30 minutes.
Then remove it, using the foil handles.
Now, prepare the lemon sauce by melting the butter in a pan.
Then add all the remaining ingredients one by one.
Once it starts boiling, that means it is done
You serve it with the egg lemon sauce.

Nutrition Facts
Servings: 4
Per Serving% Daily Value*
Calories 662
Total Fat 25.7g   33%
Saturated Fat 9.9g   50%
Trans Fat 0g
Cholesterol 392mg   143%
Sodium 580mg   25%
Potassium 1106mg   24%
Total Carb 22.3g 7%
Dietary Fiber 1.8g   6%
Sugars 3.2g
Protein 79.9g
Vitamin A 12% · Vitamin C 20%
Calcium 7% · Iron 251%
*Based on a 2,000 calorie diet

6. Pork Stew with Prunes

Preparation Time: 30 Minutes
Yield: 6 Servings

Ingredients
2 pounds of boneless pork loin
8 ounces of pitted prunes
2 cups of chicken broth
1 zest lemon
1–2 teaspoons of lemon juice
Salt and pepper
And 4 cups of warm couscous

Directions
Mix all the ingredients in an instant pot
Cover and cook it on a low pressure for 20 minutes.
Thereafter turn the heat to a high pressure and cook it for 10 minutes.
Quickly release the steam thereafter.
And serve.

Nutrition Facts
Servings: 6
Per Serving% Daily Value*
Calories 757
Total Fat 6.7g   9%
Saturated Fat 2.1g   11%
Trans Fat 0.1g
Cholesterol 110mg   40%
Sodium 354mg   15%
Potassium 1189mg   25%
Total Carb 114.8g38%
Dietary Fiber 8.7g   31%
Sugars 14.9g
Protein 56.9g
Vitamin A 10% · Vitamin C 10%
Calcium 5% · Iron 20%
*Based on a 2,000 calorie diet

7. Teriyaki Chicken Wings

Preparation Time: 20 Minutes
Yield: 5 Servings

Ingredients
4 pounds of chicken wings
11/2 cups of stevia
1 cup of soy sauce
4 tablespoons of hoisin sauce
1/3 teaspoon of grounded ginger
1 teaspoon of garlic powder
And 1 tablespoon of toasted parsley

Directions
Mix all the ingredients in an instant pot
Cover and cook it on a low pressure for 20 minutes.
Quickly release the steam.
And serve.

Nutrition Facts
Servings: 5
Per Serving % Daily Value*
Calories 747
Total Fat 27.4g   35%
Saturated Fat 7.5g   37%
Trans Fat 0g
Cholesterol 323mg   118%
Sodium 3394mg 148%
Potassium 1020mg   22%
Total Carb 10.1g 3%
Dietary Fiber 0.9g   3%
Sugars 4.5g
Protein 108.7g
Vitamin A 9% · Vitamin C 2%
Calcium 5% · Iron 31%
*Based on a 2,000 calorie diet

8. Country-Style Ribs with Sauce

Preparation Time: 20 Minutes
Yield: 4 Servings

Ingredients
3 pounds of country-style pork ribs
10 Oz. of Plum sauce
1/2 cup of stevia
2 tablespoons of soy sauce
2 tablespoons of cornstarch
1/3 cup of orange juice
Then salt and pepper

Directions
Pour the ribs and the remaining listed ingredients in an instant pot.
Cover and cook it on a high pressure for 20 minutes.
Quickly release the steam.
And serve.

Nutrition Facts
Servings: 4
Per Serving % Daily Value*
Calories 590
Total Fat 12.5g   16%
Saturated Fat 4.1g   20%
Trans Fat 0.1g
Cholesterol 248mg   90%
Sodium 645mg   28%
Potassium 1751mg   37%
Total Carb 26.4g 9%
Dietary Fiber 2.4g   9%
Sugars 19.4g
Protein 90.9g
Vitamin A 17% · Vitamin C 54%
Calcium 2% · Iron 24%
*Based on a 2,000 calorie diet

9. Moroccan Lamb Stew

Preparation Time: 25 Minutes
Yield: 4 Servings

Ingredients
2 pounds of boneless lean leg of lamb
1 cup of free chicken broth
1 and 1/2 cup of onions and tomatoes
4 large cloves of minced garlic
1 teaspoon of minced ginger root
1/3 teaspoon of ground cinnamon
1/3 teaspoon of ground turmeric
And 1 bay leaf

Garnishes
1/2 cup of raisins
Salt and pepper
1 cup of a whole almonds, toasted
2 chopped hard-boiled eggs
And a Couscous, side servings

Directions
Mix all the ingredients in an instant pot
Cover and cook it on a low pressure for 25 minutes.
Then quickly release steam.
Remove the bay leaf.
Garnish it with the raisins, and sprinkle the salt and pepper.
Then serve it with eggs and almonds over the couscous.

Nutrition Facts
Servings: 4
Per Serving % Daily Value*
Calories 1616
Total Fat 60.3g   77%
Saturated Fat 17.9g   89%
Trans Fat 0g
Cholesterol 673mg   245%

Sodium 684mg 30%
Potassium 3018mg 64%
Total Carb 54.4g 18%
Dietary Fiber 8.4g 30%
Sugars 18.9g
Protein 206.1g
Vitamin A 4% · Vitamin C 21%
Calcium 15% · Iron 92%
*Based on a 2,000 calorie diet

10. Meat Goulash

Preparation Time: 20 Minutes
Yield: 4 Servings

Ingredients
1 pound of lean pork loin
½ cup of beef broth
1 can of diced tomatoes
2 tablespoons of tomato paste
4 Oz. of divided mushrooms
2 cups of chopped onions
2 cloves of minced garlic
2 tablespoons of paprika
½ teaspoon of fennel seeds
2 bay leaves
½ cup of reduced-fat sour cream
Then salt and pepper

Side servings
1 pound of noodles, side serving (not included in Nutritional information)

Directions
Mix all ingredients in an instant pot excluding the sour cream.
Cover and cook it for 20 minutes.
Quickly release the steam.
Then remove the bay leaf.

Pour in the sour cream.
And serve it on top of the noodles.

Nutrition Facts
Servings: 4
Per Serving % Daily Value*
Calories 352
Total Fat 17.3g	22%
Saturated Fat 7.7g	39%
Trans Fat 0g
Cholesterol 102mg	37%
Sodium 182mg	8%
Potassium 900mg	19%
Total Carb 13.2g	4%
Dietary Fiber 3.7g	13%
Sugars 5.3g
Protein 36.3g
Vitamin A 85% · Vitamin C 27%
Calcium 7% · Iron 18%
*Based on a 2,000 calorie diet

Chapter 4: 14 Days Meal Plan

Developing a perfect and effective meal plan takes time, some degrees of consideration and planning to some extent too. This is because one ought to have a clearer vision and idea about what he/she wants in order to reach his goal in weight loss. Having a huge collection of recipes doesn't make the job complete, because you still need to evaluate some certain things before reaching your goal, like when going to the grocery store, one needs to focus on his/her diet plan, and this needs to be done effectively in order to save time, money and also get the desired results. It is strongly advisable that when going to a grocery store one should always endeavor to buy things from the low Carb vegetable and fruits section regardless of the prices. So as long as you have a plan to follow, you are not free to include any another item into it, in other words for you to achieve your desired goals you need to be disciplined. As a human you will at some point be tempted to alter the meal plan a little, but please bear in mind that a little swerve from the appropriate meal plan matters almost as much, no matter how small you take in.

If you have a plan to follow, then do not let the public advertisement deceive you, because in an effort to achieve your goal at its finest, you ought to have a menu plan, and also need to show all amount of consistency towards it for an effective outcome in weight loss. Below are some points, which one needs to address when going out for shopping during his/her 14-day meal plan:

- Grab the shopping list and try to get the best quality of items for your money.
- Thoroughly reading the recipe and having the list of ingredients you need for that week or day.
- Making sure you have enough to make up for the week needs.
- Making sure you spend within your allocated budget.
- Being efficient and fast.

While shopping, be positively selective by always picking the most organic, natural, preservative free, low Carb and suitable ingredients for cooking. The ingredients play a very crucial role in making a delicious yet healthy meal that contributes positively to the weight loss process.

The Main Aim of Writing This Chapter

- To involve the whole family in cooking the low Carb meals.
- Making some delicious and low Carb recipe that would be ready in a few minutes using an instant pot.
- To introduce the new and diversified collection of recipes for the two weeks.
- To introduce the recipes that is approved by the whole family.
- To encourage the use of organic ingredients as much as possible.
- Excluding added sugar, artificial flavor and additive colors.

In the previous chapter, we already categorized the recipes in such a way that you could access the ingredient easily. Along with that, the nutritional information for each recipe was provided to keep your calorie intake on track.

Useful Tips for the 2 Weeks Meal Plan Preparation

- Always use a clean stove, kitchen, and utensils.
- Wash the organic fruits and vegetables thoroughly.
- Use clean appliances and equipment.
- Always use microwave safe cups, mugs, bowls, and glasses.
- Use a heat-proof spatula.
- Use clean, odor-free and washed instant pot.

(2-weeks) 14 Days Meal Plan

The two-week meal plan provides breakfast, lunch, dinners and dessert recipes for the complete 14 days. The Carb amount is also mentioned which is often less than 130 grams per day. All the recommendations are linked to the recipes pages so that readers can finds it easy to access.
So, let's begin!

Day 1
Total Carb for the Day: 44 .8

Breakfast	P25. Egg Muffins with Vegetables
Lunch	P44. Instant Pot Squash Soup
Dinner	P119. Meat Goulash
Dessert	P98. Gingerbread Cake

Day 2
Total Carb for the Day: 98.5 g

Breakfast	P26. Savory Breakfast Muffins
Lunch	P87. Fish and Tomato Stew
Dinner	P118. Moroccan Lamb Stew
Dessert	P107. Winter Fruit Compote

Day 3
Total Carb for the Day: 117 approx

Breakfast	P28. Yummy Breakfast
Lunch	P91. Pork And Squash Ragout
Dinner	P110. Three-Meat Goulash
Dessert	P98. Gingerbread Cake

Day 4
Total Carb for the Day: 101.6

Breakfast	P33. Avocado Bread
Lunch	P88. Instant Pot Fettuccine with Seafood
Dinner	P111. Family Beef Stew
Dessert	P105. Baked Apples

Day 5
Total Carb for the Day: 52.6

Breakfast	P25. Egg Muffins with Vegetables
Lunch	P89. Shrimp and Vegetable Stew
Dinner	P112. Plain Meat Loaf
Dessert	P104. Rhubarb-Strawberry Compote

Day 6
Total Carb for the Day: 126.1

Breakfast	P31. Delicious Pancake in Instant Pot
Lunch	P66. Zucchini Casserole Recipe
Dinner	P113. Lemon Meat Loaf
Dessert	P103. Lemon Cream Cheese Bites

Day 7
Total Carb for the Day: 49.8

Breakfast	P32. Eggs and Bacon Cups
Lunch	P90. Slow-Cooker Pork Chops
Dinner	P112. Plain Meat Loaf
Dessert	P105. Baked Apples

Day 8
Total Carb for the Day: 55.7 g

Breakfast	P33. Avocado Bread 错误！未定义书签。
Lunch	P92. Ginger Pumpkin Chicken Soup
Dinner	P113. Lemon Meat Loaf
Dessert	P98. Gingerbread Cake

Day 9
Total Carb for the Day: 122.5 g

Breakfast	P35. Scramble Egg in Instant Pot
Lunch	P94. Curry-Spiced Nuts
Dinner	P112. Plain Meat Loaf
Dessert	P106. Chocolate Fondue

Day 10
Total Carb for the Day: 123.4 g

Breakfast	P36. Instant Pot Berries and Cream Breakfast Cake
Lunch	P95. Eggplant Caviar
Dinner	P116. Teriyaki Chicken Wings
Dessert	P102. Easy Brownies

Day 11
Total Carb for the Day: 121 g

Breakfast	P39. Breakfast Cobbler
Lunch	P96. Instant Pot Chicken
Dinner	P75. Chicken Adobo
Dessert	P103. Lemon Cream Cheese Bites

Day 12
Total Carb for the Day: 123. 3 g

Breakfast	P36. Instant Pot Berries and Cream Breakfast Cake
Lunch	P54. Carrot Soup
Dinner	P78. Ginger and Soy Chicken
Dessert	P99. Chocolate Chip Peanut Butter Cake

Day 13
Total Carb for the Day: 62.7

Breakfast	P40. Breakfast Porridge
Lunch	P53. Buffalo Chicken Soup
Dinner	P77. Instant Pot Beef Roast
Dessert	P98. Gingerbread Cake

Day 14
Total Carb for the Day: 58.7 g

Breakfast	P41. Simple Egg Muffins
Lunch	P56. Instant Pot Broccoli Cheddar Soup
Dinner	P76. BBQ Ribs
Dessert	P105. Baked Apples

Conclusion

The low Carb diet plan is undoubtedly the greatest key to a successful weight loss and healthier lifestyle. This book comprehensively provides the most important information on how to start a low Carb diet. All the 81 recipes mentioned in the book are part of the plan to ensure an overall smooth transition from overweight to fitness. The snippets of nutritional information for each recipe were provided as well, and also properly addressed the myth, questions and misconceptions on the low Carb diet. The book properly guides one to developing a good eating habit in order to enhance a quick adaptation to the diet plan. The book also enlightens one the effectiveness of positively selecting your purchased ingredients and how it becomes a good immunization to fighting obesity. The diet plan also helps you enjoy healthy and delicious food that will nourish your body while making you slimmer, smarter, confident, and much happier.

At the end, I want to say a very big thank you for taking your time out to read the book, hope you find it beneficial and useful.

Made in the USA
Middletown, DE
21 January 2018